ECMAScript Cookbook

Over 70 recipes to help you learn the new ECMAScript
(ES6/ES8) features and solve common JavaScript problems

Ross Harrison

BIRMINGHAM - MUMBAI

ECMAScript Cookbook

Commissioning Editor: Kunal Chaudhari
Acquisition Editor: Reshma Raman
Content Development Editor: Gauri Pradhan
Technical Editor: Leena Patil
Copy Editor: Safis Editing
Project Coordinator: Sheejal Shah
Proofreader: Safis Editing
Indexer: Tejal Daruwale Soni
Graphics: Jason Monteiro
Production Coordinator: Arvindkumar Gupta

First published: March 2018

Production reference: 1280318

Published by Packt Publishing Ltd.
Livery Place
35 Livery Street
Birmingham
B3 2PB, UK.

ISBN 978-1-78862-817-4

www.packtpub.com

To my wife Jocelyn, every day that we are together is a joy. I am truly fortunate to spend my life with you.

To my mother and brothers, thanks for dealing with me when I was young and for shaping who I am now.

To my father, "So dawn goes down today. Nothing gold can stay." I miss you.

– Ross Harrison

`mapt.io`

Mapt is an online digital library that gives you full access to over 5,000 books and videos, as well as industry leading tools to help you plan your personal development and advance your career. For more information, please visit our website.

Why subscribe?

- Spend less time learning and more time coding with practical eBooks and Videos from over 4,000 industry professionals

- Improve your learning with Skill Plans built especially for you

- Get a free eBook or video every month

- Mapt is fully searchable

- Copy and paste, print, and bookmark content

PacktPub.com

Did you know that Packt offers eBook versions of every book published, with PDF and ePub files available? You can upgrade to the eBook version at `www.PacktPub.com` and as a print book customer, you are entitled to a discount on the eBook copy. Get in touch with us at `service@packtpub.com` for more details.

At `www.PacktPub.com`, you can also read a collection of free technical articles, sign up for a range of free newsletters, and receive exclusive discounts and offers on Packt books and eBooks.

Contributors

About the author

Ross Harrison discovered programming while he was an undergraduate at the University of Nebraska-Lincoln. His first programming class was a MATLAB class that was required for mechanical engineering. Despite bombing the class, he decided that it was a lot more fun than looking at CAD. He switched to computer science the next semester and never looked back. He has worked as a software engineer for over 10 years. Most of that time has been spent creating tools for digital publishers.

I would like to thank my colleagues at Condé Nast, and John Paul, for getting me started on this process. I would like to thank all of the great people I've worked with at Condé Nast, Rowan Technology, and 42 (Walrus!). I've been lucky enough to work on some pretty cool projects with some really awesome people. I've learned a lot about software and life.

About the reviewers

Mehul Mohan was born in New Delhi, India, and is completing his education on the Goa Campus at BITS, Pilani as a CSE undergraduate. He is fascinated by programming and the fact that simple programming instructions can perform the most complex calculations known to humans. He primarily works with the MEAN stack. He is the owner of a YouTube channel called codedamn, where he presents screencasts about various programming languages. He has also received many awards from companies such as Google, Microsoft, and Sony through their responsible disclosure programs. He has also authored *Learn ECMAScript - Second Edition*, which covers ES8 and earlier versions in depth.

I'd like to thank my family and friends for making everything possible!

Kazuki Muta works at a small start-up called Mobilus Corporation, which provides a real-time communication platform and messaging system called MobiAgent.

As a JavaScript engineer, he develops React.js-based web applications and Node.js-based server-side applications.

I am grateful to Takeharu Oshida, for providing me with the opportunity to join this project, and for giving me a lot of technical advice.

Rodrigo Oler is a software engineer with a bachelor's degree in information systems from the University of Franca. He currently works at the a start-up Clubinvest as the lead mobile engineer and principal solutions architect. He also works with several start-ups promoting acceleration in technology products, building robust and high-performance solutions. He has been working with JavaScript since 2012. You can visit him on his website @rodrigooler.tk.

I thank all my family, friends and colleagues for their support and dedication, and for the incredible moments together.

Packt is searching for authors like you

If you're interested in becoming an author for Packt, please visit `authors.packtpub.com` and apply today. We have worked with thousands of developers and tech professionals, just like you, to help them share their insight with the global tech community. You can make a general application, apply for a specific hot topic that we are recruiting an author for, or submit your own idea.

Table of Contents

Preface

JavaScript permeates the development landscape like few languages before it. Since the introduction of the Node.js run-time in May of 2009, it has ventured far beyond the browser. It now works with controllers on a Raspberry Pi, as the scripting language for 3D video games that run on desktop computers, running web servers that serve millions of page views a day, and, of course, it is the dominant language for web browsers. It is possible that JavaScript is the most important programming language in the world.

The ECMAScript standard has been around almost as long as JavaScript. However, in the last few years, it has seen a flurry of activity. ES6, published in 2015, created an almost completely new language. Since then, the updates have been more gradual, but still significant. This book covers the standard up to ES8 (released in 2017). We'll discuss how to use some of its new features to organize programs more effectively and write better code.

Who this book is for

This book is intended for a broad array of readers. While this should not be considered an introductory text, anyone who has written a JavaScript program and has run it in a browser will be sufficiently prepared to read this book. JavaScript experts will also find some good food for thought.

What this book covers

Chapter 1, *Building with Modules*, covers how to use ECMAScript modules to organize code and how to configure modern browsers to use them. This chapter also covers compatibility with Google's Chrome and Mozilla's Firefox browser, and how to make them work with modules.

Chapter 2, *Staying Compatible with Legacy Browsers*, covers how to convert code that uses ECMAScript modules into a format that can be used by platforms that don't support them. We use webpack, a common JavaScript compilation tool, to assemble our modules into a single JavaScript file (called a bundle) and load it into our browser when ECMASript modules aren't compatible.

Chapter 3, *Working with Promises*, covers how to use the Promise API to organize asynchronous programs. We'll take a look at how to propagate results through promise chains and handle errors. Promises are generally regarded as an improvement over the older callback pattern. This chapter also lays a foundation for the topic covered in the next chapter.

Chapter 4, *Working with async/await and Functions*, covers how to use the new `async` and `await` features. Building on the preceding chapter, we'll take a look at how they can be replaced or used in concert with the Promise API, improving program readability while maintaining compatibility.

Chapter 5, *Web Workers, Shared Memory, and Atomics*, covers the web APIs that can be used to process data in parallel. This chapter is emblematic for the recent development of JavaScript as a language and web browsers as platforms. Parallel programming is a new domain for JavaScript that brings new possibilities and problems to the language.

Chapter 6, *Plain Objects*, demonstrates the use of API and syntax options to work with plain objects. We'll look at how to work with objects as a collection and how to define properties with some interesting behaviors.

Chapter 7, *Creating Classes*, covers the use of ECMAScript class semantics. We'll create new classes with behaviors that are defined on single instances and whole classes. We'll take a look at how to add properties and define methods.

Chapter 8, *Inheritance and Composition*, builds on our knowledge from the preceding chapter; we'll combine classes into larger structures. We'll also take a look at how to use both composition and inheritance to share behaviors between classes, and we'll discuss the benefits and drawbacks of each.

Chapter 9, *Larger Structures with Design Patterns*, further expanding on the prior two chapters, looks at some common ways that programs are organized for certain tasks. We'll implement some common design patterns and demonstrate how we can expand and modify them for different uses.

Chapter 10, *Working with Arrays*, covers the use of the new `Array` API features. In the past, working with arrays meant a lot of loops and keeping track of indices, or importing bulky libraries to clean repeated code. This chapter will show some new, functionally inspired, methods that make working with these collections much easier.

`Chapter 11`, *Working with Maps and Symbols*, covers how to make use of the `Map` and `WeakMap` classes to create relationships between different kinds of values. In this chapter, we'll look at how to use the APIs of these two classes, how they are different, and how we can control which types go into them.

`Chapter 12`, *Working with Sets*, demonstrates the use of the `Set` and `WeakSet` classes. These classes are excellent when the order of elements doesn't matter, and we just want to is something exists. We'll see how to use the APIs of these two classes, when to use one over the other, and how we can control what types go into them.

To get the most out of this book

This book assumes that you have some very basic knowledge and resources in order to get the most out of it:

- A computer with permission to install programs and configure browsers
- A text editor you are comfortable with; there are a lot of options to choose from:
  - VSCode
  - Atom
  - Vim
  - Emacs
- Some basic programming knowledge. If you haven't written a function before, this might not be the best place to start.

Download the example code files

You can download the example code files for this book from your account at `www.packtpub.com`. If you purchased this book elsewhere, you can visit `www.packtpub.com/support` and register to have the files emailed directly to you.

You can download the code files by following these steps:

1. Log in or register at `www.packtpub.com`.
2. Select the **SUPPORT** tab.
3. Click on **Code Downloads & Errata**.
4. Enter the name of the book in the **Search** box and follow the onscreen instructions.

Once the file is downloaded, please make sure that you unzip or extract the folder using the latest version of:

- WinRAR/7-Zip for Windows
- Zipeg/iZip/UnRarX for Mac
- 7-Zip/PeaZip for Linux

The code bundle for the book is also hosted on GitHub at `https://github.com/ECMAScript-Cookbook`. In case there's an update to the code, it will be updated on the existing GitHub repository.

We also have other code bundles from our rich catalog of books and videos available at `https://github.com/PacktPublishing/`. Check them out!

Conventions used

There are a number of text conventions used throughout this book.

`CodeInText`: Indicates code words in text, database table names, folder names, filenames, file extensions, pathnames, dummy URLs, user input, and Twitter handles. Here is an example: "Next, in the same directory, create a file called `hello.js`, which exports a function named `sayHi`, which writes a message to the console."

A block of code is set as follows:

```
// hello.js
export function sayHi () {
  console.log('Hello, World');
}
```

When we wish to draw your attention to a particular part of a code block, the relevant lines or items are set in bold:

```
import rocketName, { launch, COUNT_DOWN_DURATION } from './saturn-
v.js';
import falconName, { launch as falconLaunch, COUNT_DOWN_DURATION as
falconCount } from './falcon-heavy.js';
```

Any command-line input or output is written as follows:

```
cd ~/Desktop/es8-cookbook-workspace
```

Bold: Indicates a new term, an important word, or words that you see onscreen. For example, words in menus or dialog boxes appear in the text like this. Here is an example: "Double-click **nvm-setup**."

 Warnings or important notes appear like this.

 Tips and tricks appear like this.

Sections

In this book, you will find several headings that appear frequently (*Getting ready, How to do it..., How it works..., There's more...,* and *See also*).

To give clear instructions on how to complete a recipe, use these sections as follows:

Getting ready

This section tells you what to expect in the recipe and describes how to set up any software or any preliminary settings required for the recipe.

How to do it...

This section contains the steps required to follow the recipe.

How it works...

This section usually consists of a detailed explanation of what happened in the previous section.

There's more...

This section consists of additional information about the recipe in order to make you more knowledgeable about the recipe.

See also

This section provides helpful links to other useful information for the recipe.

Get in touch

Feedback from our readers is always welcome.

General feedback: Email `feedback@packtpub.com` and mention the book title in the subject of your message. If you have questions about any aspect of this book, please email us at `questions@packtpub.com`.

Errata: Although we have taken every care to ensure the accuracy of our content, mistakes do happen. If you have found a mistake in this book, we would be grateful if you would report this to us. Please visit `www.packtpub.com/submit-errata`, selecting your book, clicking on the Errata Submission Form link, and entering the details.

Piracy: If you come across any illegal copies of our works in any form on the internet, we would be grateful if you would provide us with the location address or website name. Please contact us at `copyright@packtpub.com` with a link to the material.

If you are interested in becoming an author: If there is a topic that you have expertise in and you are interested in either writing or contributing to a book, please visit `authors.packtpub.com`.

Reviews

Please leave a review. Once you have read and used this book, why not leave a review on the site that you purchased it from? Potential readers can then see and use your unbiased opinion to make purchase decisions, we at Packt can understand what you think about our products, and our authors can see your feedback on their book. Thank you!

For more information about Packt, please visit `packtpub.com`.

Building with Modules

1

In this chapter, we will cover the following recipes:

- Installing and configuring browsers—Chrome and Firefox
- Installing Python, using SimpleHTTPServer to host a local static file server
- Creating an HTML page that loads an ECMAScript module
- Exporting/importing multiple modules for external use
- Renaming imported modules
- Nesting modules under a single namespace

Introduction

JavaScript is the most famous language that adheres to the ECMAScript standard. This standard was created in the late 1990s in order to guide the development of the language. In the early years, development was slow, with only four major versions reaching production in the first two decades. However, with increased exposure, largely thanks to the popularization of the Node.js run-time, the pace of development has increased dramatically. The years 2015, 2016, and 2017 each saw new releases of the of the standard, with another planned for 2018.

With all these developments, now is an exciting time to be a JavaScript developer. A lot of new ideas are coming in from other languages, and the standard API is expanding to be more helpful. This book focuses on new features and techniques that can be used in the newer versions of JS as well as future versions!

Historically, creating JavaScript programs that span multiple files has been a painful experience. The simplest approach was to include each of the files in separate `<script>` tags. This also requires developers to position the tags in the correct order.

Various libraries have attempted to improve this situation. RequireJS, Browserfy, and Webpack all attempt to solve the problem of JavaScript dependencies and module loading. Each of these requires some kind of configuration or build step.

The situation has improved in recent years. Browser manufacturers collaborate in creating the ECMAScript specification. It is then up to the manufacturers to implement JavaScript interpreters (programs that actually run the JavaScript) that adhere to that specification

New versions of browsers are being released that support native ECMAScript modules. ECMAScript modules provide an elegant method for including dependencies. Best of all, unlike the previous methods, modules don't require any build step or configuration.

The recipes in this chapter focus on installing and configuring the Chrome and Firefox web browsers and how to take full advantage of ES modules and the import/export syntax.

Installing and configuring - Chrome

Subsequent recipes will assume an environment that is capable of using ES modules. There are two strategies for accomplishing this: creating a build step that collects all the modules used into a single file for the browser to download, or using a browser that is capable of using ES modules. This recipe demonstrates the latter option.

Getting ready

To step through this recipe, you need a computer with an operating system (OS) that is supported by Chrome (not Chromium). It supports recent versions of Windows and macOS, as well as a large number of Linux distributions. Most likely, if your OS doesn't support this browser, you are already aware of this.

How to do it...

1. To download Chrome, navigate your browser to the following:
   `https://www.google.co.in/chrome/`.
2. Click **Download** and accept the terms of service.
3. After the installer finishes downloading, double-click the installer to launch it and follow the onscreen instructions.

4. To check the version of Chrome, open the Chrome browser, and enter the following URL:
   `chrome://settings/help.`

5. You should see the **Version** number where the number is 61 or higher. See the following screenshot:

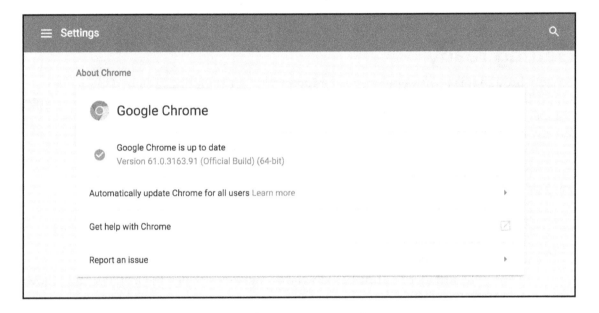

How it works...

The current versions of Chrome come with ES modules enabled out of the box. So no configuration or plugins are required to get them working!

There's more...

At the time of writing, only a few browsers support ECMAScript. You can see which browsers support modules under the **Browser compatibility** section of the page at `https://mzl.la/1PY7nnm.`

Installing and configuring - Firefox

Subsequent recipes will assume an environment that is capable of using ES modules. There are two strategies for accomplishing this: creating a build step that collects all the modules used into a single file for the browser to download, or using a browser that is capable of using ES modules. This recipe demonstrates the latter option.

Getting ready

To step through this recipe, you need a computer with an operating system (OS) that is supported by Firefox. It supports recent versions of Windows and macOS, as well as a large number of Linux distributions. Most likely, if your OS doesn't support Firefox, you are already aware of this.

How to do it...

1. To install Firefox, open a browser and enter the following URL: `https://www.mozilla.org/firefox`.
2. Click the button that says **Download** to download the installer.
3. After the installer has finished downloading, double click the installer and follow the onscreen instructions.
4. To configure Firefox, open the Firefox browser and enter the following URL: `about:config`.
5. The menu will allow you to enable advanced and experimental features. If you see a warning, click the button that says **I accept the risk!**
6. Find the **dom.moduleScripts.enabled** setting, and double-click it to set the value to **true,** as shown in following screenshot:

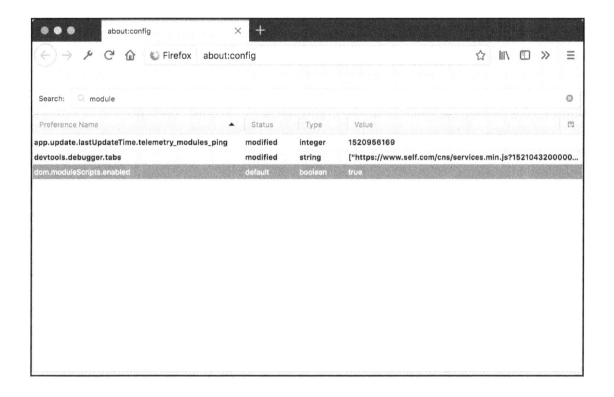

How it works...

Firefox supports ES modules, but disables them by default. This allows developers to experiment with the feature, while the majority of users are not exposed to it.

There's more...

The same as the *Installing and configuring - Chrome* section.

Installing Python, using SimpleHTTPServer to host a local static file server

It is possible to browse web pages directly from the filesystem. However, Chrome and Firefox have security features that make this inconvenient for development. What we need is a simple static file server. This recipe demonstrates how to install Python (if necessary) and use it to serve files from a directory.

Getting ready

Find out how to open the command line on your OS. On macOS and Linux, this is called the Terminal. On Windows, it is called the Command Prompt.

You should use a browser that is configured to load ES modules (see the first recipe).

How to do it...

1. Check whether you have Python installed already.
2. Open the command line.
3. Enter the following command:

   ```
   python --version
   ```

4. If you see an output like the one displayed as follows, Python is already installed. And you can skip to *step 6*:

   ```
   Python 2.7.10
   ```

5. If you receive an error such as the following, continue with the installation in *step 5*:

   ```
   command not found: python
   ```

6. Install Python on your computer:
    - For macOS, download and run the installer for the latest version of Python 2 or 3 from the following link: `https://www.python.org/downloads/mac-osx/`
    - For Windows, download and run the installer for the latest version of Python 2 or 3 from the following link: `https://www.python.org/downloads/windows/`
    - For Linux, use the operating system's built in the package manager to install the Python package
7. Create a folder on your desktop named `es8-cookbook-workspace`.
8. Inside the folder, create a text file named `hello.txt` and save some text to it.
9. Open the Command Prompt and navigate to the folder:
10. In the Linux or macOS Terminal enter:

```
cd ~/Desktop/es8-cookbook-workspace
```

11. On Windows type the following command:

```
cd C:Desktopes8-cookbook-workspace
```

12. Start the Python HTTP server with the following command:

```
python -m SimpleHTTPServer # python 2
```

Or we can use following command:

```
python -m http.server # python 3
```

13. Open your browser and enter the following URL: `http://localhost:8000/`.

14. You should see a page that shows the contents of the es8-cookbook-workspace folder:

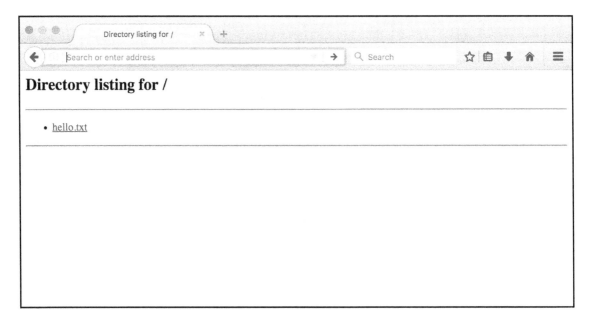

15. Click on the link to **hello.txt** and you'll see the text contents of the file you created.

How it works...

The first thing we did was check if Python was installed. The best way to do this is to ask Python for its version number. This way we know whether Python is installed, and if it's new enough for our purposes.

If it's not installed, Python can be retrieved via the OS's package manager, or via the installers made available through Python's website.

Once installed, Python comes with a lot of utilities. The one we are interested in is the appropriately named SimpleHTTPServer. This utility listens for HTTP requests on port 8000, and returns the contents of the files relative to the directory root. If the path points to a directory, it returns an HTML page that lists the directory contents.

Creating an HTML page that loads an ECMAScript module

In previous recipes, we went over installation and configurations instructions to run a static file server using Python and configure a browser to use ES modules.

Getting ready

This recipe assumes that you have the static file server running in your working directory. If you haven't installed Python or configured your browser to work with ES modules, please see the first two recipes in the book.

The following steps will demonstrate how to create an ES module and load it into an HTML file.

How to do it...

1. Create an `hello.html` file with a some text content:

```html
<html>
 <meta charset="UTF-8" />
  <head>
  </head>
  <body>
  Open Your Console!
  </body>
</html>
```

2. Open `hello.html` by opening your browser, and entering the following URL: `http://localhost:8000/hello.html`.

3. You should see **Open Your Console!** displayed by the browser:

4. Lets do what the page tells us and open up the Developer Console. For both Firefox and Chrome, the command is the same:
    - On Windows and Linux:

        Ctrl + Shift + I

    - On macOS:

        Cmd + Shift + I

5. Next, in the same directory, create a file called `hello.js`, which exports a function named `sayHi` that writes a message to the console:

```
// hello.js
export function sayHi () {
  console.log('Hello, World');
}
```

6. Next add a script module tag to the head of `hello.html` that imports the `sayHi` method from `hello.js` (pay attention to the type value).

7. Reload the browser window with the Developer Console open and you should see the `hello` message displayed as text:

How it works...

Although our browser can work with ES modules, we still need to specify that is how we want our code to be loaded. The older way of including script files uses `type="text/javascript"`. This tells the browser to execute the content of the tag immediately (either from tag contents or from the `src` attribute).

By specifying `type="module"`, we are telling the browser that this tag is an ES module. The code within this tag can import members from other modules. We imported the function `sayHi` from the `hello` module and executed it within that `<script>` tag. We'll dig into the `import` and `export` syntax in the next couple of recipes.

See also

- *Exporting/importing multiple modules for external use*
- *Adding fallback script tags*

Exporting/importing multiple modules for external use

In the previous recipe, we loaded an ES module into an HTML page and executed an exported function. Now we can take a look at using multiple modules in a program. This allows us more flexibility when organizing our code.

Getting ready

Make sure you have Python installed and your browser properly configured.

How to do it...

1. Create a new working directory, navigate into it with your command-line application, and start the Python `SimpleHTTPServer`.

2. Create a file named `rocket.js` that exports the name of a rocket, a countdown duration, and a launch function:

```
export default name = "Saturn V";
export const COUNT_DOWN_DURATION = 10;


export function launch () {
  console.log(`Launching in ${COUNT_DOWN_DURATION}`);
  launchSequence();
}

function launchSequence () {
  let currCount = COUNT_DOWN_DURATION;

  const countDownInterval = setInterval(function () {
    currCount--;

    if (0 < currCount) {
      console.log(currCount);
    } else {

      console.log('LIFTOFF!!! 🚀 ');
      clearInterval(countDownInterval);
    }
  }, 1000);
```

```
}
```

3. Create a file named `main.js` that imports from `rocket.js`, logs out details, and then calls the launch function:

```
import rocketName, {COUNT_DOWN_DURATION, launch } from
'./rocket.js';

export function main () {
  console.log('This is a "%s" rocket', rocketName);
  console.log('It will launch in  "%d" seconds.',
COUNT_DOWN_DURATION);
  launch();
}
```

4. Next, create an `index.html` file that imports the `main.js` module and runs the `main` function:

```
<html>
  <head>
    <meta charset='UTF-8' />
  </head>
  <body>
    <h1>Open your console.</h1>
    <script type="module">
      import { main } from './main.js';
      main();
    </script>
  </body>
</html>
```

5. Open your browser and then the `index.html` file. You should see the following output:

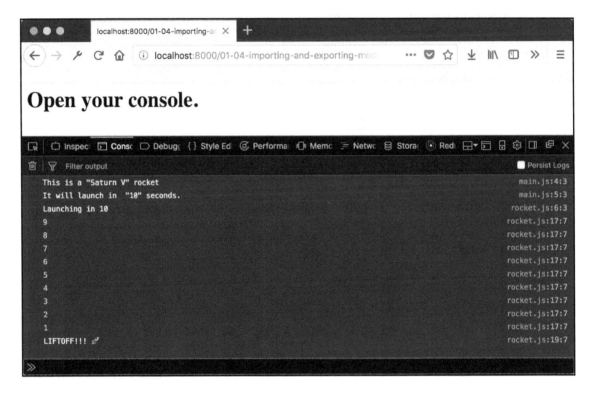

How it works...

There are two options for exporting a member from a module. It can either be exported as the `default` member, or as a named member. In `rocket.js`, we see both methods:

```
export default name = "Saturn V";
export const COUNT_DOWN_DURATION = 10;
export function launch () { ... }
```

In this case, the string `"Saturn V"` is exported as the default member, while `COUNT_DOWN_DURATION` and `launch` are exported as named members. We can see the effect this has had when importing the module in `main.js`:

```
import rocketName, { launch, COUNT_DOWN_DURATION } from './rocket.js';
```

We can see the difference in how the default member and the name members are imported. The name members appear inside the curly braces, and the name they are imported with matches their name in the module source file. The default module, on the other hand, appears outside the braces, and can be assigned to any name. The unexported member `launchSequence` cannot be imported by another module.

See also

- *Renaming imported modules*
- *Nesting imported modules under a single namespace*

Renaming imported modules

Modules allow more flexibility in organizing code. This allows for a shorter, more contextual name. For example, in the previous recipe, we named a function `launch` instead of something more verbose such as `launchRocket`. This helps keep our code more readable, but it also means that different modules can export members that use the same name.

In this recipe, we'll rename imports in order to avoid these namespace collisions.

Getting ready

We'll be reusing the code from the previous recipe (*Exporting/importing multiple modules for external use*). The changes from the previous files will be highlighted.

How to do it...

1. Copy the folder created for the previous recipe into a new directory.
2. Navigate to that directory with your command-line application and start the Python server.

3. Rename `rocket.js` to `saturn-v.js`, add the name of the rocket to the log statements, and update the `main.js` import statement:

```
// main.js
import name, { launch, COUNT_DOWN_DURATION } from './saturn-v.js';

export function main () {
  console.log('This is a "%s" rocket', name);
  console.log('It will launch in  "%d" seconds.',
COUNT_DOWN_DURATION);
  launch();
}
// saturn-v.js
export function launch () {
  console.log(`Launching %s in ${COUNT_DOWN_DURATION}`, name);
  launchSequence();
}

function launchSequence () {
  // . . .

      console.log(%shas LIFTOFF!!! 🚀 ', name); // . . . }
```

4. Copy `saturn-v.js` to a new file named `falcon-heavy.js` and change the default export value and the `COUNT_DOWN_DURATION`:

```
export default name = "Falcon Heavy";
export const COUNT_DOWN_DURATION = 5;
```

5. Import the `falcon` module into `main.js`. Rename the imported members to avoid conflicts and launch the falcon rocket as well:

```
import rocketName, { launch, COUNT_DOWN_DURATION } from './saturn-
v.js';
import falconName, { launch as falconLaunch, COUNT_DOWN_DURATION as
falconCount } from './falcon-heavy.js';

export function main () {
  console.log('This is a "%s" rocket', rocketName);
  console.log('It will launch in  "%d" seconds.',
COUNT_DOWN_DURATION);
  launch();
  console.log('This is a "%s" rocket', falconName);
console.log('It will launch in  "%d" seconds.', falconCount);
falconLaunch();
}
```

6. Open `index.html` in your browser and you should see the following output:

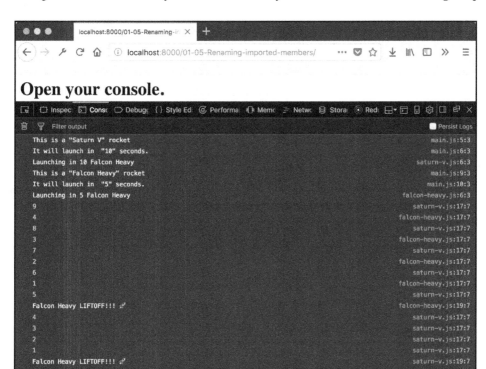

How it works...

When we duplicated the `saturn-v.js` file to and imported the members from `falcon-heavy.js`, we had a potential namespace conflict. Both files export members named `COUNT_DOWN_DURATION` and launch. But using the `as` keyword, we renamed those members in order to avoid that conflict. Now the importing `main.js` file can use both sets of members without issue.

Renaming members can also be helpful to adding context. For example, it might be useful to rename the launch as `launchRocket` even if there is no conflict. This give the importing module additional context, and makes the code a bit clearer.

Nesting modules under a single namespace

As the number of modules grows, patterns start to emerge. For practical and architectural reasons, it makes sense to group multiple modules together and use them as a single package.

This recipe demonstrates how to collect multiple modules together and use them as a single package.

Getting ready

It will be helpful to have the source code available from previous recipes to bootstrap this recipe. Otherwise, you'll need to reference *Exporting/importing multiple modules for external use* for how to create the index.html file.

How to do it...

1. Create a new folder with an index.html file, as seen in *Exporting/importing multiple modules for external use*.
2. Inside of that directory, create a folder named rockets.
3. Inside of rockets, create three files: falcon-heavy.js, saturn-v.js, and launch-sequence.js:

```
// falcon-heavy.js
import { launchSequence } from './launch-sequence.js';

export const name = "Falcon Heavy";
export const COUNT_DOWN_DURATION = 5;

export function launch () {
  launchSequence(COUNT_DOWN_DURATION, name);
} (COUNT_DOWN_DURATION);
}

// saturn-v.js
import { launchSequence } from './launch-sequence.js';

export const name = "Saturn V";
export const COUNT_DOWN_DURATION = 10;

export function launch () {
```

```
    launchSequence(COUNT_DOWN_DURATION, name);
}

// launch-sequence.js
export function launchSequence (countDownDuration, name) {
  let currCount = countDownDuration;
  console.log(`Launching in ${COUNT_DOWN_DURATION}`, name);

  const countDownInterval = setInterval(function () {
    currCount--;

    if (0 < currCount) {
      console.log(currCount);
    } else {

      console.log('%s LIFTOFF!!!      ', name);
      clearInterval(countDownInterval);
    }
  }, 1000);
}
```

4. Now create `index.js`, which exports the members of those files:

```
import * as falconHeavy from './falcon-heavy.js';
import * as saturnV from './saturn-v.js';
export { falconHeavy, saturnV };
```

5. Create a `main.js` file (in the folder that contains `rockets`), which imports `falconHeavey` and `saturnV` from the `index.js` file and launches them:

```
import { falconHeavy, saturnV } from './rockets/index.js'

export function main () {
  saturnV.launch();
  falconHeavy.launch();
}
```

6. Open in the browser, and see the following output:

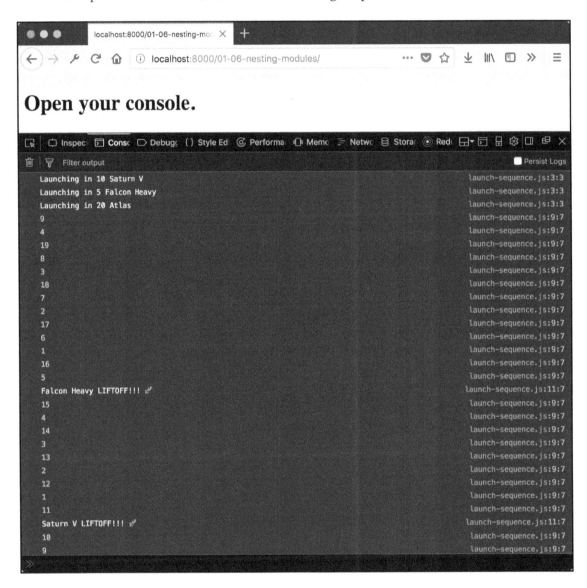

How it works...

The * syntax seen on the first two lines of index.js imports all the exported members under the same object. This means that the name, COUNT_DOWN_DURATION, and launch members of falcon-heavey.js are all attached to the falconHeavy variable. Likewise, for the saturn-v.js modules and the saturnV variable. So, when falconHeavy and saturnV are exported on *line 4*, those exported names now contain all the exported members of their respective modules.

This provides a single point where another module (main.js in this case) can import those members. The pattern has three advantages. It is simple; there is only one file to import members from, rather than many. It is consistent, because all packages can use an index module to expose members of multiple modules. It is more flexible; members of some modules can be used throughout a package and not be exported by the index module.

There's more...

It is possible to export named items directly. Consider the following file, atlas.js:

```
import { launchSequence } from './launch-sequence.js';

const name = 'Atlas';
const COUNT_DOWN_DURATION = 20;

export const atlas = {
  name: name,
  COUNT_DOWN_DURATION: COUNT_DOWN_DURATION,
  launch: function () {
    launchSequence(COUNT_DOWN_DURATION, name);
  }
};
```

The atlas member can be exported directly by index.js:

```
import * as falconHeavy from './falcon-heavy.js';
import * as saturnV from './saturn-v.js';

export { falconHeavy, saturnV };
export { atlas } from './atlas.js';
```

Then the `main.js` file can import the `atlas` member and launch it:

```
import { atlas, falconHeavy, saturnV } from './rockets/index.js'

export function main () {
  saturnV.launch();
  falconHeavy.launch();
  atlas.launch();
}
```

This is one benefit of always using named exports; it's easier to collect and export specific members from packages with multiple modules.

Whether named or not, nesting is a great technique for grouping modules. It provides a mechanism for organizing code as the number of modules continues to grow.

2
Staying Compatible with Legacy Browsers

In this chapter, we will cover the following recipes:

- Installing Node.js with NVM
- Installing and configuring webpack
- Adding fallback script tags to load client bundles
- Shimming methods with Babel Polyfill
- Supporting new language features with Babel
- Using tools to analyze webpack bundles

Introduction

In the preceding chapter, we covered how to take advantage of the new ECMAScript modules to load code from multiple files and organize our code. This cutting-edge technique has only recently become available in browsers. In practice, production websites try to target as many users as possible. This often means targeting older browsers. In addition, JavaScript also runs in other environments (such as Node.js) that do not support ECMAScript modules.

The good news is that we don't have to change our source code in order to support these platforms. There are tools available that produce a single JavaScript file from multiple source files. This way we can use modules to organize our code, and run our programs on more platforms.

The recipes in this chapter focus on installation and configuration of webpack in order to provide a fallback option for platforms that don't support ES modules and other more recent additions to the language.

Installing Node.js with NVM – Linux and macOS

Node provides installation binaries for Windows and macOS on its website: `https://nodejs.org/en/download/`.

It's easy to install Node.js by downloading the appropriate installer for your OS and processor. However, it is useful to have a version manager so that you can work on projects that require different versions, and use the latest version. This is especially useful if your package manager doesn't provide a recent version of Node.js (for example, Ubuntu).

Subsequent recipes will assume that Node.js is installed. This recipe demonstrates how to install Node.js for Linux and macOS. The next recipe will cover the installation instructions for Windows.

Getting ready

This recipe is only for Linux and macOS. See the next recipe for Windows instructions.

You must have git installed. This comes installed on macOS, and Linux distributions should provide git through their package managers.

How to do it...

1. Open your command-line application.
2. Clone the `nvm` project into a directory in your home folder:

```
git clone https://github.com/creationix/nvm.git ~/.nvm
```

3. Add the following code to the bottom of your ~/.bashrc or ~/.zshrc file. If you don't know what shell you are running, it is probably bash and you should add the entry to ~/.bashrc:

```
# Configure NVM
export NVM_DIR="$HOME/.nvm"
[ -s "$NVM_DIR/nvm.sh" ] && . "$NVM_DIR/nvm.sh"
[ -s "$NVM_DIR/bash_completion" ] && . "$NVM_DIR/bash_completion"
```

4. Save the file and return to your command line:

```
source ~/.bashrc # (or ~/.zshrc if you're running zshell)
```

5. Confirm your installation by checking the version number of nvm:

```
> nvm --version
0.33.5
```

6. List all of the node versions available for installation:

```
> nvm list-remote
```

7. Install the latest **Long Term Support** (**LTS**) or stable version. (At the time of writing, version 8.9.4 is the latest LTS version):

```
> nvm install 8.9.4
```

8. Confirm the installation of node and npm by checking their version numbers:

```
>   node --version
v8.9.4
> npm --version
5.6.0
```

How it works...

The keys to this installation are *step 4* and *step 5*. The *step 4* ensures that the nvm executable is part of your environment's PATH, and the associated environment variables are set. When you run nvm install 6.11, the nvm executable is run, and the node binaries are installed to the expected location.

There's more...

If we have also installed version v9.6.1, we would use the following command to set it as the default:

```
nvm alias default 9.6.1
```

Now when we open a new shell, v9.6.1 will be the Node.js version in use.

Installing Node.js with NVM: Windows

Subsequent recipes will assume that Node.js is installed. This recipe demonstrates how to install Node.js for Windows.

Getting ready

This recipe is meant for the Windows environment. See the previous recipe for macOS and Linux instructions.

You must also have git installed. You can download git from the following link:

```
https://git-scm.com/download/win.
```

How to do it...

1. Visit the project release page:
   `https://github.com/coreybutler/nvm-windows/releases`.
2. Download the latest `nvm-setup.zip` file.
3. Extract the downloaded ZIP.
4. Double-click **nvm-setup**.
5. Go through the wizard to complete the installation.
6. Open the Command Prompt.
7. Confirm the installation by checking the version number of `nvm`:

```
> nvm version
1.1.6
```

8. List all of the Node.js versions available for installation:

```
> nvm list available
```

9. Install the latest LTS or stable version (at time of writing, version 8.9.4 is the latest LTS version):

```
> nvm install 8.9.4
6.11.0
Downloading node.js version 8.9.4 (64-bit)...
Complete
Creating C:UsersrtharAppDataRoamingnvmtemp
Downloading npm version 5.6.0... Complete
Installing npm v5.6.0...
Installation complete.
```

10. Enter the following command to activate this version:

```
nvm use 8.9.6
```

How it works...

The installation downloads the installation wizard. The installation wizard downloads the executable files associated with nvm, and adjusts the PATH environment variable. The PATH is used to look up programs when they are executed on the command line. If a program is in one of the folders found in the PATH, then it can be executed without referencing its absolute or relative path.

There's more...

If we have also installed version v9.6.1, we would use the following command to set it as the default:

```
nvm use 9.6.1
```

Now when we open a new shell, v8.6.0 will be the Node.js version in use. Unlike the macOS and Linux versions, the last version selected is maintained through shell sessions, and a default doesn't need to be set.

Installing and configuring webpack

As mentioned before, there are a few options for creating JavaScript bundles. Rollup and Babel are popular tools that can perform this task. The webpack is a good option because it is widely used and has a large plugin base.

This recipe demonstrates how to install and configure webpack to build a JavaScript bundle.

Getting ready

You'll need to have Node.js installed. If not, please see the appropriate recipe for installing Node.js with nvm.

How to do it...

1. Open your command-line application, navigate to your workspace, and create a new node package:

```
mkdir 02-creating-client-bundles
cd 02-creating-client-bundles
npm init -y
```

2. Duplicate the main.js file from the *Nesting modules under a single namespace* recipe in Chapter 1, *Building with Modules*:

```
// main.js
import { atlas, saturnV } from './rockets/index.js'

export function main () {
  saturnV.launch();
  atlas.launch();
}
```

4. Create the rockets dependencies directory (these files can be copied from *Nesting modules under a single namespace* recipe in Chapter 1, *Building with Modules*):

```
// rockets/index.js
import * as saturnV from './saturn-v.js';
import * as atlas from './atlas.js';
export { saturnV, atlas };
```

```
// rockets/launch-sequence.js
export function launchSequence (countDownDuration, name) {
  let currCount = countDownDuration;
  console.log(`Launching in ${countDownDuration}`, name);

  const countDownInterval = setInterval(function () {
    currCount--;

    if (0 < currCount) {
      console.log(currCount);
    } else {
      console.log('%s LIFTOFF!!! 🚀', name);
      clearInterval(countDownInterval);
    }
  }, 1000);
}

// rockets/atlas.js
import { launchSequence } from './launch-sequence.js';

const name = 'Atlas';
const COUNT_DOWN_DURATION = 20;

export function launch () {
  launchSequence(COUNT_DOWN_DURATION, name);
}

// rockets/saturn-v.js
import { launchSequence } from './launch-sequence.js';

export const name = "Saturn V";
export const COUNT_DOWN_DURATION = 10;

export function launch () {
  launchSequence(COUNT_DOWN_DURATION, name);
}
```

5. Create an index.js file that loads and executes the main function from main.js:

```
// index.js
import { main } from './main.js';
main();
```

6. Install webpack:

```
> npm install --save-dev Webpack
```

7. Create a webpack configuration file, named `webpack.config.js`, with an entry point at `index.js` and this output filename: `bundle.js`:

```
// webpack.config.js
const path = require('path');

module.exports = {
  entry: './index.js',
  output: {
    filename: 'bundle.js',
    path: path.resolve(__dirname)
  }
};
```

8. Add a build script to `package.json`:

```
{
  /** package.json content**/
  "scripts": {
    "build": "webpack --config webpack.config.js"
  }
}
```

9. Run the webpack build to create `bundle.js`:

```
> npm run build
```

10. You should see output that describes the build created and the modules contained therein. See the following output:

```
Hash: 5f2f1a7c077186c7a7a7
Version: webpack 3.6.0
Time: 134ms
     Asset    Size  Chunks             Chunk Names
bundle.js  6.7 kB       0  [emitted]  main
   [0] ./rockets/launch-sequence.js 399 bytes {0} [built]
   [1] ./index.js 42 bytes {0} [built]
   [2] ./main.js 155 bytes {0} [built]
   [3] ./rockets/index.js 162 bytes {0} [built]
   [4] ./rockets/falcon-heavy.js 206 bytes {0} [built]
   [5] ./rockets/saturn-v.js 203 bytes {0} [built]
   [6] ./rockets/atlas.js 270 bytes {0} [built]
```

11. Run the produced `bundle.js` file with `node`:

```
node ./bundle.js
```

12. You should see the rockets count down and blast off.

How it works...

Installing webpack with `npm` downloads the published package to the `node_modules` directory. Because webpack also includes an executable, it is installed under `node_modules/.bin`.

The webpack configuration is fairly simple. It specifies an entry point and an output. The entry point defines where webpack begins its traversal. Next, it visits all the modules that are imported by the entry point and then all the modules imported by those. This is repeated until all the dependencies have been visited.

Then all the dependencies are merged into a single file. The file location is defined by the output settings. In this case, the output is defined as `bundle.js`. The output bundles are placed in the current directory.

 You can visit the webpack docs for more detail on how it works and how to configure it for different scenarios at: `https://webpack.js.org/`.

Adding fallback script tags to load client bundles

In the previous recipe, we showed how to combine multiple modules with webpack. This recipe demonstrates how to load these into browsers that don't support ES modules.

Getting ready

This recipe assumes that you have webpack installed and configured. It is suggested that you complete the previous recipe, *Installing and configuring webpack*, before continuing with this recipe.

You will also need to have Python installed. If you haven't yet, visit the *Installing Python, using* `SimpleHTTPServer` *to host a local static file server* recipe in `Chapter 1`, *Building with Modules*.

How to do it...

1. Open your command-line application and navigate to the directory containing the `02-creating-client-bundles` package.
2. Start the Python HTTP server.
3. Create a file named `index.html` (copied from the *Nesting modules under a single namespace* recipe in `Chapter 1`, *Building with Modules*):

```
<html>
  <head>
    <meta charset='UTF-8' />
  </head>
  <body>
    <h1>Open your console.</h1>
    <script type="module">
      import { main } from './main.js';
      main();
    </script>
  </body>
</html>
```

4. Add a `nomodule` script tag to the body after the existing `module` in the `<script>` tag:

```
<body>
  <h1>Open your console.</h1>
  <script type="module">
    import { main } from './main.js';
    main();
  </script>
  <script nomodule type="text/javascript"src="bundle.js"></script>
</body>
```

5. Run the `webpack` build command:

```
./node_modules/.bin/webpack --config webpack.config.js
```

6. Open your ES module-compatible browser, open the Developer tools to the
Network tab, and visit the URL:
`http://localhost:8000/`.

7. You should see the individual files loaded by the browser:

8. Open a browser that isn't compatible with ES modules. Open the Developer tools
to **Network** and visit the URL:
`http://localhost:8000/`.

9. You should see the `bundle.js` file loaded instead:

How it works...

We saw in previous recipes that a script tag with the attribute `type="module"` will be executed and treated like an ES module. Browsers that don't support ES modules will not execute this script at all.

If we were to insert a normal script tag, it would be executed by newer browsers as well. In order to avoid running duplicated code we use the `nomodule` attribute. This tells newer browsers that support ES modules to ignore ID.

Thus, we get the desired behavior. The module tags are executed by compatible browsers and ignored by older browsers. `nomodule`-attributed scripts are ignored by ES module-compatible browsers and executed by legacy browsers.

 At the time of writing, `nomodule` is an experimental feature and is not supported by all browsers. However, it may be supported in the future.

See also

- Shimming newer features with Babel

Shimming methods with Babel Polyfill

In the previous two recipes, we saw how to create a client bundle and load it into a browser. This make it possible to use ES modules in source code without breaking compatibility with older browsers.

However, there are also new methods available in newer versions of the language that we'll be using in later chapters.

This recipe demonstrates how to use the `babel-polyfill` library to support those methods.

Getting ready

This recipe assumes that you have the code created in earlier recipes in this chapter, and that you have installed Python and know how to start the static HTTP server. Please visit the earlier recipes or copy the code.

How to do it...

1. Open your command line application and navigate to the directory containing the `02-creating-client-bundles` package.
2. Start the Python HTTP server.
3. Update the `main.js` file to use the `Array.prototype.values` method, and use `for..of` to loop over the resulting iterator:

```
import { atlas, saturnV } from './rockets/index.js'

export function main () {
  const rockets = [saturnV, atlas];
  for (const rocket of rockets.values()) {
    rocket.launch();
  }
}
```

4. Install the Babel Polyfill package:

```
npm install --save babel-polyfill
```

5. To shim the bundle, update the `webpack.config.js` file to add Babel Polyfill to the entry point:

```
const path = require('path');

module.exports = {
  entry: ['babel-polyfill', './index.js'],
  output: {
    filename: 'bundle.js',
    path: path.resolve(__dirname)
  }
};
```

6. To shim ES modules, you'll need to import the file directly. Update `index.html` to import the polyfill:

```
<!-- index.html -->
<script type="module">
  import './node_modules/babel-polyfill/dist/polyfill.min.js';
  import { main } from './main.js';
  main();
</script>
```

7. Now open a browser, open the Developer Console, and visit the URL: `http://localhost:8000/`.

8. Whether the browser supports `Array.prototype.values` or not, the code should run and display output as follows:

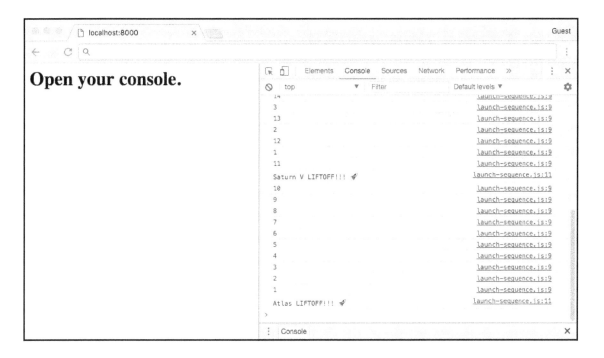

How it works...

The `babel-polyfill` package, appropriately enough, provides what are known as polyfills. A polyfill fills in the gaps that legacy browsers leave in the ECMAScript spec.

In the previous example, it just so happens that the current version, 61, of Chrome does not implement the `Array.prototype.values` method. The polyfill code runs before the main function. It looks to see if the `values` method is implemented on the `Array.prototype` object. If it isn't implemented natively, then polyfill implements the method. If it is implemented then polyfill leaves the native implementation in place.

In this way, the polyfill library makes a large set of newer methods available.

Supporting new language features with Babel

In the previous recipe, we saw how to use the `babel-polyfill` library to support new ES methods. This add methods to the language at runtime, so that source code that depends on them runs correctly.

There are other language features that are relatively new to ECMAScript, such as the arrow function, **let** and **const** variable declarations, and spread operators. These features are not universally supported. Babel provides a mechanism to use them at the source level, and remain compatible with a build step.

This recipe demonstrates how to use Babel within webpack, in order to support these features in older browsers.

Getting ready

This recipe assumes that you have the code created in earlier recipes in this chapter, and that you have installed Python. Please visit these earlier recipes or copy the code.

How to do it...

1. Open your command-line application and navigate to the directory containing the `02-creating-client-bundles` package.
2. Start the Python HTTP server.
3. Update the `main.js` file to use the arrow function syntax:

```
import { atlas, saturnV } from './rockets/index.js'

export function main () {
  const rockets = [saturnV, atlas];
  rockets.map((rocket) => rocket.launch() );
}
```

4. Install Babel, the `preset-es2015`, and the associated webpack loader:

```
npm install --save-dev babel-cli babel-preset-es2015 babel-loader
```

5. Create a Babel configuration file named `.babelrc`:

```
// .babelrc
{
   "presets": ["es2015"]
}
```

6. Configure `webpack` to use Babel for transpiling new language features:

```
const path = require('path');

module.exports = {
   entry: ['babel-polyfill', './index.js'],
   output: {
      filename: 'bundle.js',
      path: path.resolve(__dirname)
   }, module: {
      rules: [
         {
            test: /.js$/,
            exclude: /node_modules/,
            use: 'babel-loader'
         }
      ]
   }
};
```

7. Add a webpack build command to the script section of the `package.json` file:

```
{
   /* package.json configuration */

   "scripts": {
      "bundle": "webpack --config webpack.config.js",
   }

   /* remaining properties */
}
```

8. Run the `webpack` build:

```
npm run bundle
```

9. Now, open a browser and open the Developer Console while visiting the URL: `http://localhost:8000/`.

10. You should see the code running correctly:

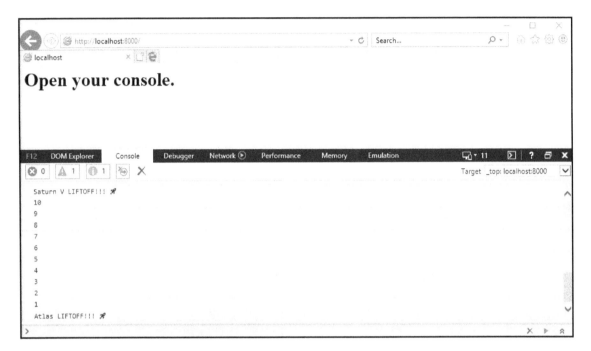

How it works...

The Babel project provides a compiler, commonly known as a **transpiler**. A transpiler is a program that ingests source code and produces some target code. The most common use for the Babel transpiler is to take JavaScript source files and translate newer features.

When the transpiler sees an expression that uses a language feature that needs to be translated, it produces a logically equivalent expression. The produced expressions can be very similar, or very different from the source expression.

 For more details on how to use Babel to support different platforms, look at its website at:
https://babeljs.io/.

There's more...

The previous recipe uses the ES2015 preset. This means that Babel will always produce ES2015 (ES5)-compatible code regardless of current browser support.

The Babel `env` preset is more sophisticated, and uses platform compatibility to determine which language features need to be translated. See the following example from the project readme:

```
// .baberc
{
  "presets": [
    ["env", {
    "targets": {
      "browsers": ["last 2 versions", "safari >= 7"]
    }
  }]
    ]
}
```

The preceding configuration targets the last two version of all browsers except Safari, which is targeted all the way back to version 7. This project allows Babel to discard translations that are no longer needed as browsers implement more language features.

> You can find more documentation and support for the `babel-preset-env` project at its repository at: `https://github.com/babel/babel-preset-env`.

Using tools to analyze webpack bundles

A major disadvantage of transpiling and using Polyfills is that the source code can diverge quite dramatically from the source code. This can often result in bloated bundle sizes. If you look at the file size of the `bundle.js` file after the Polyfill library was added (see the previous two recipes), then you'll see that it is over 200Kb. This is quite large when compared to 5Kb without the Polyfill.

With many bundles, it is difficult to find out what files are responsible for the large file size, and what the dependencies are between them.

In this recipe, we will see how to use analysis tools to get a better perspective on our webpack bundles.

Getting ready

It will be helpful to have the source code available from previous recipes to bootstrap this recipe. Otherwise, you'll need to reference *Exporting/importing multiple modules for external use* recipe from `Chapter 1`, *Building with Modules*, for how to create the `index.html` file.

How to do it...

1. Open your command-line application and navigate to the directory containing the `02-creating-client-bundles` package.
2. Run the webpack and output the profile output to a JSON file:

```
./node_modules/.bin/webpack --config webpack.config.js  --profile -
-json > compilation-stats.json
```

3. To see which modules are taking up the most space in your bundle, open your browser and visit the URL:
   `https://chrisbateman.github.io/webpack-visualizer/`.
4. Drag and drop the file or use the file selector to select **compilation-stats.json**.
5. You should see a chart that will give you hoverable module size information:

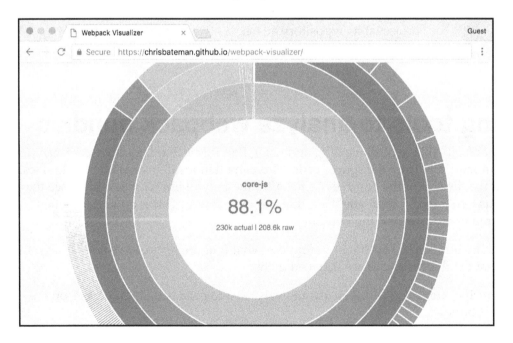

6. Now that you know which modules are large, you can look for the dependencies. Visit the webpack analyzer homepage at: `https://webpack.github.io/analyse/`.

7. Drag and drop the file or use the file selector to select **compilation-stats.json**.

8. You should see the interface change after it loads the file. Click on the **Modules** line in the header.

9. From here, you can see individual modules and where the dependencies are:

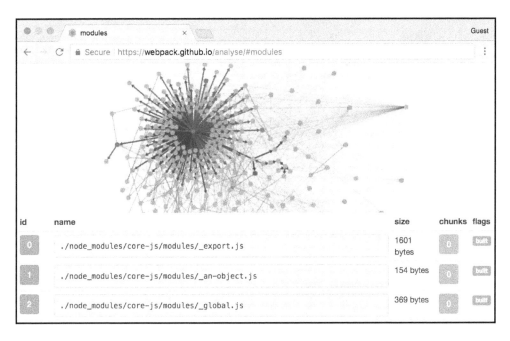

How it works...

In *step 2*, we ran the webpack command and output statistics in a JSON file. This data includes information such as file size contribution and dependencies. The sites we opened up read that JSON data and produced a visualization. The first site, WEBPACK VISUALIZER (`https://chrisbateman.github.io/webpack-visualizer/`), uses the file size data and emphasizes how much each package contributes to the overall bundle size. This is useful for identifying the culprits when it comes to inflated bundle sizes.

Unfortunately, removing a large dependency isn't always easy. Dependencies can be multiple levels-deep and difficult to find. Once we know what is contributing to large bundle sizes, then we can use the second tool, Webpack Visualizer, to extract them.

Working with Promises

3

In this chapter, we will cover the following recipes:

- Creating and waiting for Promises
- Resolving Promise results
- Rejecting Promise errors
- Chaining Promises
- Starting a Promise chain with Promise.resolve
- Using Promise.all to resolve multiple Promises
- Handling errors with Promise.catch
- Simulating finally with the Promise API

Introduction

In earlier versions of JavaScript, the callback pattern was the most common way to organize asynchronous code. It got the job done, but it didn't scale well. With callbacks, as more asynchronous functions are added, the code becomes more deeply nested, and it becomes more difficult to add to, refactor, and understand the code. This situation is commonly known as **callback hell**.

Promises were introduced to improve on this situation. Promises allow the relationships of asynchronous operations to be rearranged and organized with more freedom and flexibility.

The recipes in this chapter demonstrate how to use promises to create and organize asynchronous functions, as well as how to handle error conditions.

Creating and waiting for Promises

Promises provide a way to compose and combine asynchronous functions in an organized and easier to read way. This recipe demonstrates a very basic usage of promises.

Getting ready

This recipe assumes that you already have a workspace that allows you to create and run ES modules in your browser. If you don't, please see the first two chapters.

How to do it...

1. Open your command-line application and navigate to your workspace.
2. Create a new folder named `03-01-creating-and-waiting-for-promises`.
3. Copy or create an `index.html` that loads and runs a `main` function from `main.js`.
4. Create a `main.js` file that creates a promise and logs messages before and after the promise is created, as well as while the promise is executing and after it has been resolved:

```js
// main.js
export function main () {

  console.log('Before promise created');

  new Promise(function (resolve) {
    console.log('Executing promise');
    resolve();
  }).then(function () {
    console.log('Finished promise');
  });

  console.log('After promise created');
}
```

5. Start your Python web server and open the following link in your browser: `http://localhost:8000/`.

6. You will see the following output:

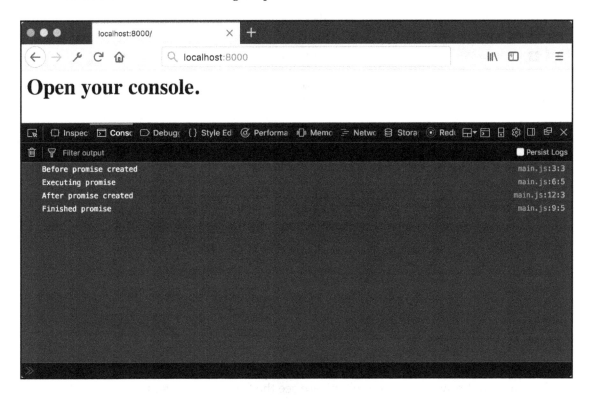

How it works...

By looking at the order of the log messages, you can clearly see the order of operations. First, the initial log is executed. Next, the promise is created with an executor method. The executor method takes `resolve` as an argument. The `resolve` function fulfills the promise.

Promises adhere to an interface named **thenable**. This means that we can chain `then` callbacks. The callback we attached with this method is executed after the `resolve` function is called. This function executes asynchronously (not immediately after the Promise has been resolved).

Finally, there is a log after the promise has been created.

The order the logs messages appear reveals the asynchronous nature of the code. All of the logs are seen in the order they appear in the code, except the `Finished promise` message. That function is executed asynchronously after the `main` function has exited!

We'll be looking more at `resolve`, `then`, and other parts of the promise API in later recipes in this chapter.

Resolving Promise results

In the previous recipe, we saw how to use promises to execute asynchronous code. However, this code is pretty basic. It just logs a message and then calls `resolve`. Often, we want to use asynchronous code to perform some long-running operation, then return that value.

This recipe demonstrates how to use `resolve` in order to return the result of a long-running operation.

Getting ready

This recipe assumes that you already have a workspace that allows you to create and run ES modules in your browser. If you don't, please see the first two chapters.

How to do it...

1. Open your command-line application and navigate to your workspace.
2. Create a new folder named `3-02-resolving-promise-results`.
3. Copy or create an `index.html` that loads and runs a `main` function from `main.js`.

4. Create a `main.js` file that creates a promise and logs messages before and after the promise is created:

```
// main.js
export function main () {

  console.log('Before promise created');

  new Promise(function (resolve) {
  });

  console.log('After promise created');
}
```

5. Within the promise, resolve a random number after a 5-second timeout:

```
new Promise(function (resolve) {
  setTimeout(function () {
    resolve(Math.random());
  }, 5000);
})
```

6. Chain a `then` call off the promise. Pass a function that logs out the value of its only argument:

```
new Promise(function (resolve) {
  setTimeout(function () {
    resolve(Math.random());
  }, 5000);
}).then(function (result) {
  console.log('Long running job returned: %s', result);
});
```

7. Start your Python web server and open the following link in your browser: `http://localhost:8000/`.

8. You should see the following output:

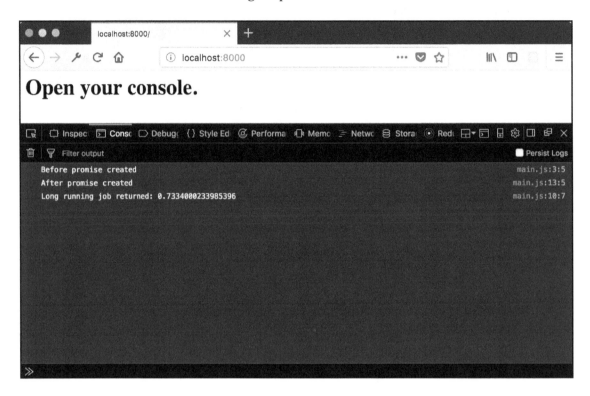

How it works...

Just as in the previous recipe, the promise was not fulfilled until `resolve` was executed (this time after 5 seconds). This time however, we passed the called `resolve` immediately with a random number for an argument. When this happens, the argument is provided to the callback for the subsequent `then` function. We'll see in future recipes how this can be continued to create *promise chains*.

Rejecting Promise errors

In the previous recipe, we saw how to use `resolve` to provide a result from a successfully fulfilled promise. Unfortunately, the code doesn't always run as expected. Network connections can be down, data can be corrupted, and uncountable other errors can occur. We need to be able to handle those situations as well.

This recipe demonstrates how to use `reject` when errors arise.

Getting ready

This recipe assumes that you already have a workspace that allows you to create and run ES modules in your browser. If you don't, please see the first two chapters.

How to do it...

1. Open your command-line application and navigate to your workspace.
2. Create a new folder named `3-03-rejecting-promise-errors`.
3. Copy or create an `index.html` that loads and runs a `main` function from `main.js`.
4. Create a `main.js` file that creates a promise, and logs messages before and after the promise is created and when the promise is fulfilled:

```
new Promise(function (resolve) {
  resolve();
  }).then(function (result) {
  console.log('Promise Completed');
});
```

5. Add a second argument to the promise callback named `reject`, and call `reject` with a new error:

```
new Promise(function (resolve, reject) {
  reject(new Error('Something went wrong');
}).then(function (result) {
console.log('Promise Completed');
});
```

6. Chain a `catch` call off the promise. Pass a function that logs out its only argument:

```
new Promise(function (resolve, reject) {
  reject(new Error('Something went wrong'));
}).then(function (result) {
console.log('Promise Completed');
}).catch(function (error) {       console.error(error);       });
```

8. Start your Python web server and open the following link in your browser: `http://localhost:8000/`.

9. You should see the following output:

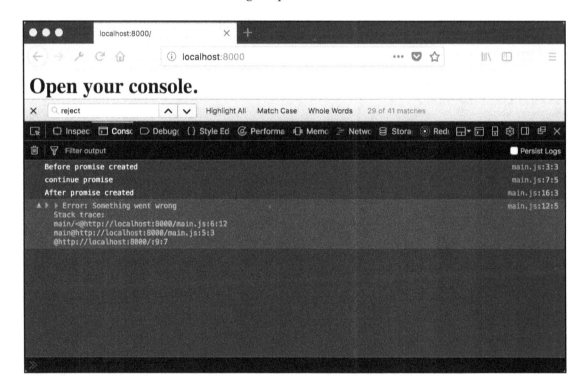

How it works...

Previously we saw how to use `resolve` to return a value in the case of a successful fulfillment of a promise. In this case we called `reject` before `resolve`. This means that the Promise finished with an error before it could `resolve`.

When the Promise completes in an error state, the `then` callbacks are not executed. Instead we have to use `catch` in order to receive the error that the Promise rejects. You'll also notice that the `catch` callback is only executed after the `main` function has returned. Like successful fulfillment, listeners to unsuccessful ones execute asynchronously.

See also

- Handle errors with `Promise.catch`
- Simulating `finally` with `Promise.then`

Chaining Promises

So far in this chapter, we've seen how to use promises to run single asynchronous tasks. This is helpful but doesn't provide a significant improvement over the callback pattern. The real advantage that promises offer comes when they are composed.

In this recipe, we'll use promises to combine asynchronous functions in series.

Getting ready

This recipe assumes that you already have a workspace that allows you to create and run ES modules in your browser. If you don't, please see the first two chapters.

How to do it...

1. Open your command-line application and navigate to your workspace.
2. Create a new folder named `3-04-chaining-promises`.
3. Copy or create an `index.html` that loads and runs a `main` function from `main.js`.

4. Create a `main.js` file that creates a promise. Resolve a random number from the promise:

```
new Promise(function (resolve) {
  resolve(Math.random());
});
);
```

5. Chain a `then` call off of the promise. Return `true` from the callback if the random value is greater than or equal to `0.5`:

```
new Promise(function (resolve, reject) {
      resolve(Math.random());
}).then(function(value) {
  return value >= 0.5;
});
```

6. Chain a final `then` call after the previous one. Log out a different message if the argument is `true` or `false`:

```
new Promise(function (resolve, reject) {
  resolve(Math.random());
}).then(function (value) {
  return value >= 0.5;
}).then(function (isReadyForLaunch) {
  if (isReadyForLaunch) {
    console.log('Start the countdown! 🚀');
  } else {
    console.log('Abort the mission. 👾');
  }
});
```

7. Start your Python web server and open the following link in your browser: `http://localhost:8000/`.

8. If you are lucky, you'll see the following output:

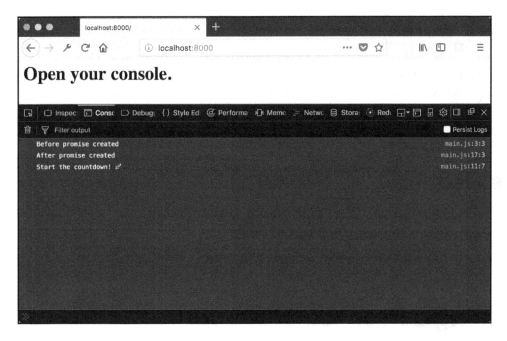

9. If you are unlucky, we'll see the following output:

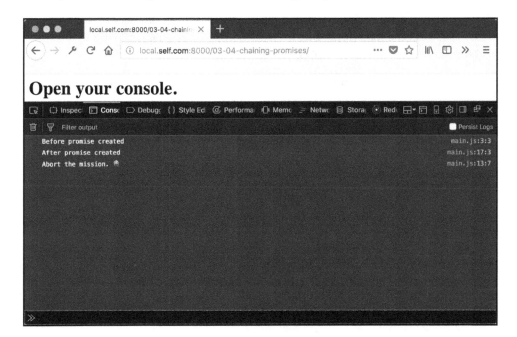

How it works...

We've already seen how to use `then` to wait for the result of a promise. Here, we are doing the same thing multiple times in a row. This is called a promise chain. After the promise chain is started with the new promise, all of the subsequent links in the promise chain return promises as well. That is, the callback of each `then` function is `resolve` like another promise.

See also

- Using `Promise.all` to resolve multiple Promises
- Handle errors with `Promise.catch`
- Simulating `finally` with a final `Promise.then` call

Starting a Promise chain with Promise.resolve

In this chapter's preceding recipes, we've been creating new `promise` objects with the constructor. This gets the jobs done, but it creates a problem. The first callback in the promise chain has a different shape than the subsequent callbacks.

In the first callback, the arguments are the `resolve` and `reject` functions that trigger the subsequent `then` or `catch` callbacks. In subsequent callbacks, the returned value is propagated down the chain, and thrown errors are captured by `catch` callbacks. This difference adds mental overhead. It would be nice to have all of the functions in the chain behave in the same way.

In this recipe, we'll see how to use `Promise.resolve` to start a promise chain.

Getting ready

This recipe assumes that you already have a workspace that allows you to create and run ES modules in your browser. If you don't, please see the first two chapters.

How to do it...

1. Open your command-line application and navigate to your workspace.
2. Create a new folder named `3-05-starting-with-resolve`.
3. Copy or create an `index.html` that loads and runs a `main` function from `main.js`.
4. Create a `main.js` file that calls `Promise.resolve` with an empty object as the first argument:

```
export function main () {
  Promise.resolve({})
}
```

5. Chain a `then` call off of `resolve`, and attach rocket boosters to the passed object:

```
export function main () {
  Promise.resolve({}).then(function (rocket) {
    console.log('attaching boosters');
    rocket.boosters = [{
      count: 2,
      fuelType: 'solid'
    }, {
      count: 1,
      fuelType: 'liquid'
    }];
    return rocket;
  })
}
```

6. Add a final `then` call to the chain that lets you know when the `boosters` have been added:

```
export function main () {
  Promise.resolve({})
    .then(function (rocket) {
      console.log('attaching boosters');
      rocket.boosters = [{
        count: 2,
        fuelType: 'solid'
      }, {
        count: 1,
        fuelType: 'liquid'
      }];
      return rocket;
    })
```

```
            .then(function (rocket) {
              console.log('boosters attached');
              console.log(rocket);
            })
        }
```

7. Start your Python web server and open the following link in your browser: `http://localhost:8000/`.

8. You should see the following output:

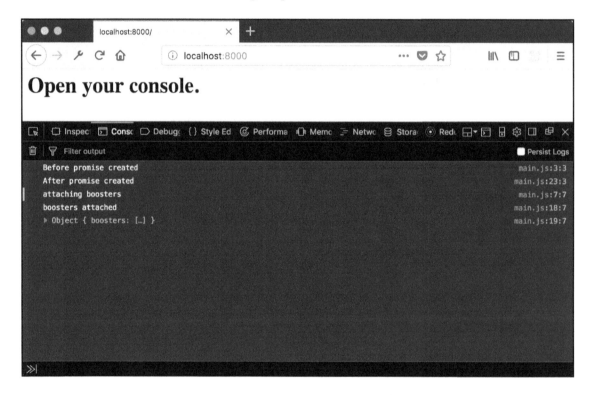

How it works...

`Promise.resolve` creates a new promise that resolves the value passed to it. The subsequent `then` method will receive that resolved value as it's argument. This method can seem a little roundabout but can be very helpful for composing asynchronous functions. In effect, the constituents of the promise chain don't need to be aware that they are in the chain (including the first step). This makes transitioning from code that doesn't use promises to code that does much easier.

Using Promise.all to resolve multiple promises

So far, we've seen how to use promises to perform asynchronous operations in sequence. This is useful when the individual steps are long-running operations. However, this might not always be the more efficient configuration. Quite often, we can perform multiple asynchronous operations at the same time.

In this recipe, we'll see how to use `Promise.all` to start multiple asynchronous operations, without waiting for the previous one to complete.

Getting ready

This recipe assumes that you already have a workspace that allows you to create and run ES modules in your browser. If you don't, please see the first two chapters.

How to do it...

1. Open your command-line application and navigate to your workspace.
2. Create a new folder named `3-06-using-promise-all`.
3. Copy or create an `index.html` that loads and runs a `main` function from `main.js`.

4. Create a `main.js` file that creates an object named `rocket`, and calls `Promise.all` with an empty array as the first argument:

```
export function main() {
  console.log('Before promise created');

  const rocket = {};
  Promise.all([])

  console.log('After promise created');
}
```

5. Create a function named `addBoosters` that creates an object with `boosters` to an object:

```
function addBoosters (rocket) {
  console.log('attaching boosters');
  rocket.boosters = [{
    count: 2,
    fuelType: 'solid'
  }, {
    count: 1,
    fuelType: 'liquid'
  }];
  return rocket;
}
```

6. Create a function named `performGuidanceDiagnostic` that returns a promise of a successfully completed task:

```
function performGuidanceDiagnostic (rocket) {
  console.log('performing guidance diagnostic');

  return new Promise(function (resolve) {
    setTimeout(function () {
      console.log('guidance diagnostic complete');
      rocket.guidanceDiagnostic = 'Completed';
      resolve(rocket);
    }, 2000);
  });
}
```

7. Create a function named `loadCargo` that adds a payload to the `cargoBay`:

```
function loadCargo (rocket) {
  console.log('loading satellite');
  rocket.cargoBay = [{ name: 'Communication Satellite' }]
  return rocket;
}
```

8. Use `Promise.resolve` to pass the `rocket` object to these functions within `Promise.all`:

```
export function main() {

  console.log('Before promise created');

  const rocket = {};
  Promise.all([
    Promise.resolve(rocket).then(addBoosters),
    Promise.resolve(rocket).then(performGuidanceDiagnostic),
    Promise.resolve(rocket).then(loadCargo)
  ]);

  console.log('After promise created');
}
```

9. Attach a `then` call to the chain and log that the rocket is ready for launch:

```
const rocket = {};
Promise.all([
  Promise.resolve(rocket).then(addBoosters),
  Promise.resolve(rocket).then(performGuidanceDiagnostic),
  Promise.resolve(rocket).then(loadCargo)
]).then(function (results) {
  console.log('Rocket ready for launch');
  console.log(results);
});
```

10. Start your Python web server and open the following link in your browser: `http://localhost:8000/`.

11. You should see the following output:

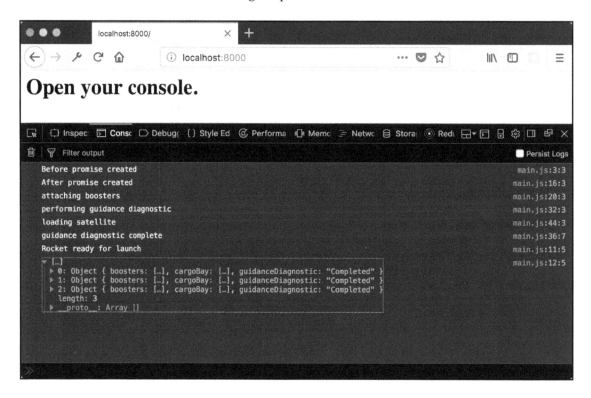

How it works...

`Promise.all` is similar to `Promise.resolve`; the arguments are resolved as promises. The difference is that instead of a single result, `Promise.all` accepts an **iterable** argument, each member of which is resolved individually.

In the preceding example, you can see that each of the promises is initiated immediately. Two of them are able to complete while `performGuidanceDiagnostic` continues. The promise returned by `Promise.all` is fulfilled when all the constituent promises have been resolved.

The results of the promises are combined into an array and propagated down the chain. You can see that three references to `rocket` are packed into the `results` argument. And you can see that the operations of each promise have been performed on the resulting object.

There's more

As you may have guessed, the results of the constituent promises don't have to return the same value. This can be useful, for example, when performing multiple independent network requests. The index of the result for each promise corresponds to the index of the operation within the argument to `Promise.all`. In these cases, it can be useful to use array destructuring to name the argument of the `then` callback:

```
Promise.all([
  findAstronomers,
  findAvailableTechnicians,
  findAvailableEquipment
]).then(function ([astronomers, technicians, equipment]) {
  // use results for astronomers, technicians, and equipment
});
```

Handling errors with Promise.catch

In a previous recipe, we saw how to fulfill a promise with an error state using `reject`, and we saw that this triggers the next `catch` callback in the promise chain. Because promises are relatively easy to compose, we need to be able to handle errors that are reported in different ways. Luckily promises are able to handle this seamlessly.

In this recipe, we'll see how `Promises.catch` can handle errors that are reported by being thrown or through rejection.

Getting ready

This recipe assumes that you already have a workspace that allows you to create and run ES modules in your browser. If you don't, please see the first two chapters.

How to do it...

1. Open your command-line application and navigate to your workspace.
2. Create a new folder named `3-07-handle-errors-promise-catch`.
3. Copy or create an `index.html` that loads and runs a `main` function from `main.js`.

4. Create a `main.js` file with a `main` function that creates an object named `rocket`:

```
export function main() {

  console.log('Before promise created');

  const rocket = {};

  console.log('After promise created');
}
```

5. Create a function `addBoosters` that throws an error:

```
function addBoosters (rocket) {
  throw new Error('Unable to add Boosters');
}
```

6. Create a function `performGuidanceDiagnostic` that returns a promise that rejects an error:

```
function performGuidanceDiagnostic (rocket) {
  return new Promise(function (resolve, reject) {
    reject(new Error('Unable to finish guidance diagnostic'));
  });
}
```

7. Use `Promise.resolve` to pass the rocket object to these functions, and chain a `catch` off each of them:

```
export function main() {

  console.log('Before promise created');

  const rocket = {};
  Promise.resolve(rocket).then(addBoosters)
    .catch(console.error);
  Promise.resolve(rocket).then(performGuidanceDiagnostic)
    .catch(console.error);

  console.log('After promise created');
}
```

8. Start your Python web server and open the following link in your browser:
   `http://localhost:8000/`.

9. You should see the following output:

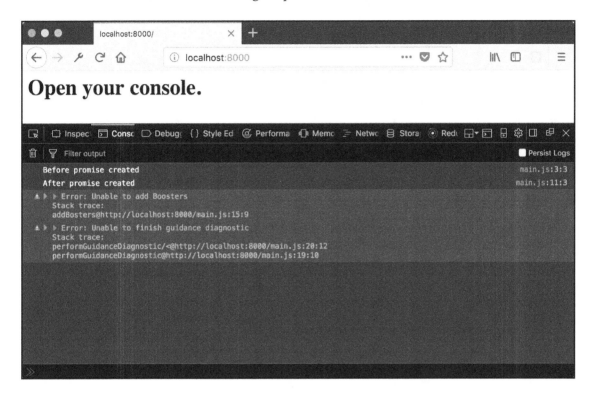

How it works...

As we saw before, when a promise is fulfilled in a rejected state, the callback of the `catch` functions is triggered. In the preceding recipe, we see that this can happen when the `reject` method is called (as with `performGuidanceDiagnostic`). It also happens when a function in the chain throws an error (as will `addBoosters`).

This has similar benefit to how `Promise.resolve` can normalize asynchronous functions. This handling allows asynchronous functions to not know about the promise chain, and announce error states in a way that is familiar to developers who are new to promises.

This makes expanding the use of promises much easier.

Simulating finally with the promise API

In a previous recipe, we saw how `catch` can be used to handle errors, whether a promise has rejected, or a callback has thrown an error. Sometimes, it is desirable to execute code whether or not an error state has been detected. In the context of `try/catch` blocks, the `finally` block can be used for this purpose. We have to do a little more work to get the same behavior when working with promises

In this recipe, we'll see how a final `then` call to execute some code in both successful and failing fulfillment states.

Getting ready

This recipe assumes that you already have a workspace that allows you to create and run ES modules in your browser. If you don't, please see the first two chapters.

How to do it...

1. Open your command-line application and navigate to your workspace.
2. Create a new folder named `3-08-simulating-finally`.
3. Copy or create an `index.html` that loads and runs a `main` function from `main.js`.
4. Create a `main.js` file with a `main` function that logs out messages for before and after promise creation:

   ```
   export function main() {

     console.log('Before promise created');

     console.log('After promise created');
   }
   ```

5. Create a function named `addBoosters` that throws an error if its first parameter is `false`:

   ```
   function addBoosters(shouldFail) {
     if (shouldFail) {
       throw new Error('Unable to add Boosters');
     }
   ```

```
    return {
      boosters: [{
        count: 2,
        fuelType: 'solid'
      }, {
        count: 1,
        fuelType: 'liquid'
      }]
    };
  }
```

6. Use `Promise.resolve` to pass a Boolean value that is `true` if a random number is greater than `0.5` to `addBoosters`:

```
export function main() {

  console.log('Before promise created');

  Promise.resolve(Math.random() > 0.5)
    .then(addBoosters)

  console.log('After promise created');
}
```

7. Add a `then` function to the chain that logs a success message:

```
export function main() {

  console.log('Before promise created');
  Promise.resolve(Math.random() > 0.5)
    .then(addBoosters)
      .then(() => console.log('Ready for launch: 🚀'))

  console.log('After promise created');
}
```

8. Add a `catch` to the chain and log out the error if thrown:

```
export function main() {
  console.log('Before promise created');
  Promise.resolve(Math.random() > 0.5)
    .then(addBoosters)
    .then(() => console.log('Ready for launch: 🚀'))
      .catch(console.error)
  console.log('After promise created');
}
```

9. Add a `then` after the `catch`, and log out that we need to make an announcement:

```
export function main() {

    console.log('Before promise created');
    Promise.resolve(Math.random() > 0.5)
      .then(addBoosters)
      .then(() => console.log('Ready for launch: 🚀'))
      .catch(console.error)
      .then(() => console.log('Time to inform the press.'));
    console.log('After promise created');
}
```

10. Start your Python web server and open the following link in your browser:
`http://localhost:8000/`.

11. If you are lucky and the boosters are added successfully, you'll see the following output:

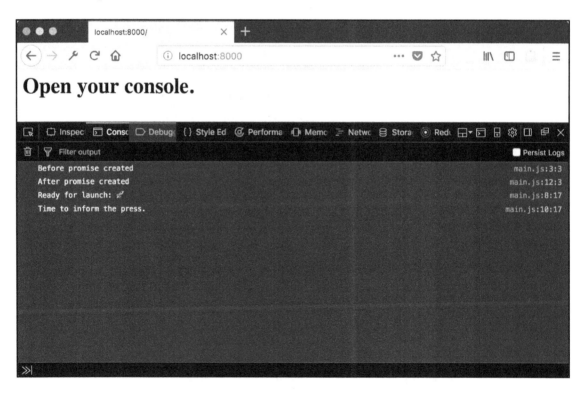

12. If you are unlucky, you'll see an error message like the following:

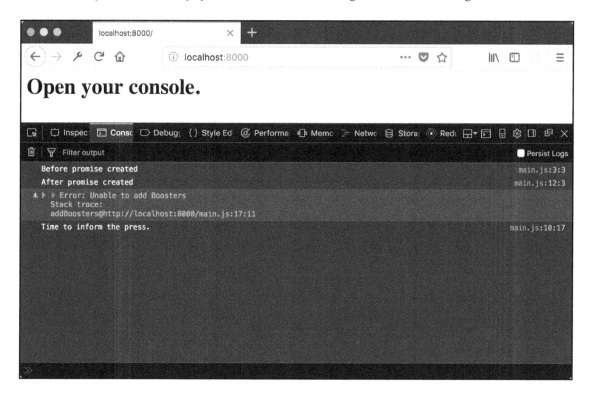

How it works...

We can see in the preceding output that whether or not the asynchronous function completes in an error state, the last `then` callback is executed. This is possible because the `catch` method doesn't stop the promise chain. It simply catches any error states from the previous links in the chain, and then propagates a new value forward.

The final `then` is then protected from being bypassed by an error state by this `catch`. And so, regardless of the fulfillment state of prior links in the chain, we can be sure that the callback of this final `then` will be executed.

Working with async/await and Functions 4

In this chapter, we will cover the following recipes:

- Creating promises with an async function
- Awaiting the result of an async function
- Using async results in a Promise chain
- Awaiting multiple results in a series
- Awaiting multiple results concurrently
- Using Promise.all to collect an array of async results
- Handling errors when awaiting an async function
- Handling errors thrown inside of Promise.all
- Using finally to ensure an operation is performed

Introduction

In the previous chapter, we saw how Promises are a huge improvement over the callback pattern. But we also saw that there were still some rough edges around composition. Creating promises directly takes different shape functions that are placed later in the chain. Errors and successful results were provided in different ways depending on how the Promise was created. And there is still be a bit of inconvenient nesting.

The `async` and `await` operators were introduced with ES8. These build on top of the Promise to make working with and creating Promises more seamless. In this chapter, we'll see how `async` and `await` can be used to create and work with promises in a more elegant way.

Creating promises with an async function

The `async` functions are an easy way to create and work with promises. In this recipe, we'll see a basic form of this.

Getting ready

This recipe assumes you already have a workspace that allows you to create and run ES modules in your browser. If you don't, please see the first two chapters.

How to do it...

1. Open your command-line application and navigate to your workspace.
2. Create a new folder named `04-01-creating-Promise-with-async`.
3. Copy or create an `index.html` that loads and runs a `main` function from `main.js`.
4. Create a `main.js` with an `async` function named `someTask`:

```
// main.js
async function someTask () {
    console.log('Performing some task');
}
```

5. Create a `main` that calls `someTask` and logs messages before and after `someTask` is executed:

```
export function main () {
  console.log('before task');
  someTask();
  console.log('after task created');
}
```

6. Chain a `then` call off of `someTask` and log a message in the callback function:

```
export function main () {
  console.log('Before Promise created');
  someTask().then(function () {
    console.log('After Task completed');
  });
  console.log('After Promise created');}
```

7. Start your Python web server and open the following link in your browser: `http://localhost:8000/`.

8. You should see the following output:

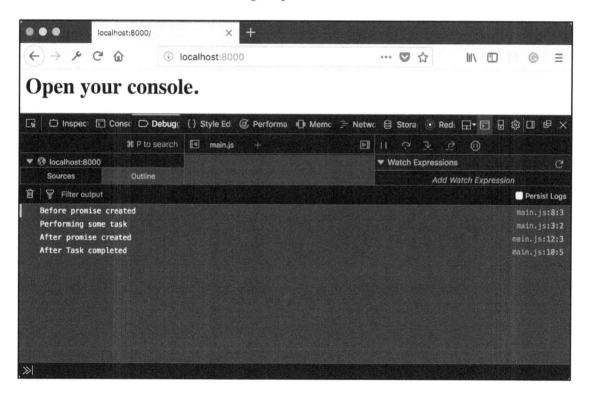

How it works...

The `async` keyword instructs the run-time that this function returns a Promise, rather than a result directly. By looking at the log messages, you can clearly see the order of operations. The first message is logged before the `async` function call is made. Next, the message inside of the `async` function is logged. Then the message after the `async` function is called. And finally, the message inside of the `then` callback is logged. This order is the same order of execution that can be seen in code using the Promise API directly.

The preceding code is already an improvement over code that creates promises directly. In upcoming recipes, we'll see how to take advantage of `await` to retrieve results from these functions without the use of the Promise API. We'll also be looking at other situations where `async` functions provide an advantage over direct use of the Promise API.

Awaiting the result of async functions

In the previous recipe, we saw how to use `async` to create functions that resolve promises. However, we used the Promise API `then` callback to wait for the result. In many situations, we can use the `await` key word to wait for these values. It gets the job done, but there is a cleaner way to retrieve results from asynchronous functions.

This recipe demonstrates how to use `await` in order to return the result of a long-running operation.

Getting ready

This recipe assumes you already have a workspace that allows you to create and run ES modules in your browser. If you don't, please see the first two chapters.

How to do it...

1. Open your command-line application and navigate to your workspace.
2. Create a new folder named `4-02-await-async-results`.
3. Copy or create an `index.html` that loads and runs a `main` function from `main.js`.

4. Create a `main.js` with an `async` function named `getRandomNumber` that returns a random number:

```
// main.js
async function getRandomNumber () {
    return Math.random();
}
```

5. Create an `async` function, `main`, that calls `getRandomNumber`, waits for the result, and logs out the value:

```
export async function main () {
  console.log('before task');
  const result = await getRandomNumber();
  console.log('Received the value: %s', result);
  console.log('after task completed');
}
```

6. Start you Python web server and open the following link in your browser: `http://localhost:8000/`.

7. You should see the following output:

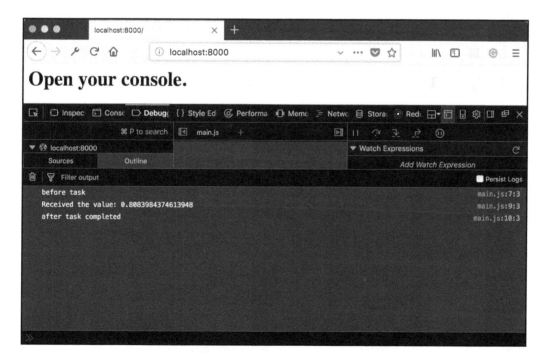

How it works...

Using `await` within an `async` function is equivalent to using `then` in a Promise chain. The difference is that instead of the result being passed as an argument to the callback function, it is resolved as an expression. This expression can be assigned to the constant `result`. The value is then available for the rest of the block, and not limited to the body of a callback function.

This is pretty cool! Previously getting results from asynchronous code required the use of callbacks and methods in the Promise API. Now, with the `async` and `await` keywords, we can write code without nesting, making it easier to read and understand, while maintaining compatibility with the Promise API.

Using async results in a Promise chain

In the previous recipe, we saw how to use `async` and `await` to replace portions of the Promise API. However, there will still be cases where it is preferable to use the Promise API, either for clarity, structure, or incremental replacement.

In this recipe, we'll see how the `async` functions integrate seamlessly into Promise chains.

Getting ready

This recipe assumes you already have a workspace that allows you to create and run ES modules in your browser. If you don't, please see the first two chapters.

How to do it...

1. Open your command-line application and navigate to your workspace.
2. Create a new folder named `04-03-async-function-Promise-chain`.
3. Copy or create an `index.html` that loads and runs a `main` function from `main.js`.

4. Create an `async` function, `getRandomNumber`, that returns a random number:

```
async function getRandomNumber() {
  console.log('Getting random number.');
  return Math.random();
}
```

5. Create an `async` function, `determinReadyToLaunch`, that returns `true` if its first argument is greater than `0.5`:

```
async function deteremineReadyToLaunch(percentage) {
  console.log('Determining Ready to launch.');
  return Math.random() > 0.5;
}
```

6. Create a third `async` function, `reportResults`, that logs out different results if its first argument is `true` or `false`:

```
async function reportResults(isReadyToLaunch) {
  if (isReadyToLaunch) {
    console.log('Rocket ready to launch. Initiate countdown: 🚀
');
  } else {
    console.error('Rocket not ready. Abort mission: ⚫');
  }
}
```

7. Create a `main` function that calls `getRandomNumber`, and a chain of the Promise it creates to call `determineReadyToLaunch` and `reportResults` in succession:

```
export function main() {
  console.log('Before Promise created');
  getRandomNumber()
    .then(deteremineReadyToLaunch)
    .then(reportResults)
  console.log('After Promise created');
}
```

8. Start your Python web server and open the following link in your browser: `http://localhost:8000/`.

9. You should see the following output:

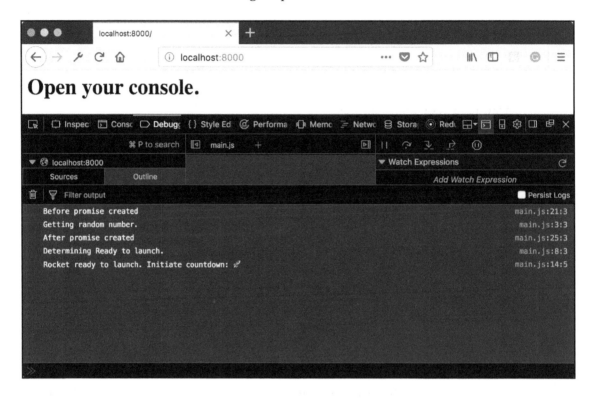

How it works...

As mentioned previously, `async` functions resolve their results with a Promise, rather than directly returning a value. This means that whether an `async` function is used to start or continue a Promise chain, the shape can be the same.

There's more...

In fact, because the results are always resolved with a Promise, `async` functions can be resolved as a group using `Promise.all`. You can see an example of `async` functions with their results joined with a `Promise.all`:

```
async function checkEngines(threshold = 0.9) {
    return Math.random() < threshold;
```

```
}

async function checkFlightPlan(threshold = 0.9) {
  return Math.random() < threshold;
}

async function checkNavigationSystem(threshold = 0.9) {
  return Math.random() < threshold;
}

Promise.all([
    checkEngines(),
    checkFlightPlan(0.5),
    checkNavigationSystem(0.75)
]).then(function([enginesOk, flighPlanOk, navigationOk]) {
  if (enginesOk) {
    console.log('engines ready to go');
  } else {
    console.error('engines not ready');
  }

  if (flighPlanOk) {
    console.log('flight plan good to go');
  } else {
    console.error('error found in flight plan');
  }

  if (navigationOk) {
    console.log('navigation systems good to go');
  } else {
    console.error('error found in navigation systems');
  }
})
```

The preceding code works as expected. The functions can even be called directly with an argument, without needing to wrap them in a call to `Promise.resolve`.

Awaiting multiple results in a series

Sometimes it's necessary to arrange asynchronous operations in a series. In previous recipes, we've seen how to do this with `Promise.then`. In this recipe, we'll see how to do the same thing with the `await` operator.

Getting ready

This recipe assumes you already have a workspace that allows you to create and run ES modules in your browser. If you don't, please see the first two chapters.

How to do it...

1. Open your command-line application and navigate to your workspace.
2. Create a new folder named `04-03-async-function-Promise-chain`.
3. Copy or create an `index.html` that loads and runs a `main` function from `main.js`.
4. Create an `async` function, `getRandomNumber`, that returns a random number:

```
async function getRandomNumber() {
  console.log('Getting random number.');
  return Math.random();
}
```

5. Create an `async` function, `determineReadyToLaunch`, that returns `true` if its first argument is greater than `0.5`:

```
async function determineReadyToLaunch(percentage) {
  console.log('Determining Ready to launch.');
  return Math.random() > 0.5;
}
```

6. Create a third `async` function, `reportResults`, that logs out different results if it's first argument is `true` or `false`:

```
async function reportResults(isReadyToLaunch) {
  if (isReadyToLaunch) {
    console.log('Rocket ready to launch. Initiate countdown: 🚀
');
  } else {
    console.error('Rocket not ready. Abort mission: 🔴');
  }
}
```

7. Create a `main` function that calls `getRandomNumber`, awaits the result, passes it on to `determineReadyToLaunch`, and calls `reportResults` after awaiting ready to launch:

```
export async function main() {
  const randomNumber = await getRandomNumber();
  const ready = await deteremineReadyToLaunch(randomNumber);
  await reportResults(ready);
}
```

8. Start your Python web server and open the following link in your browser: `http://localhost:8000/`.

9. You should see the following output:

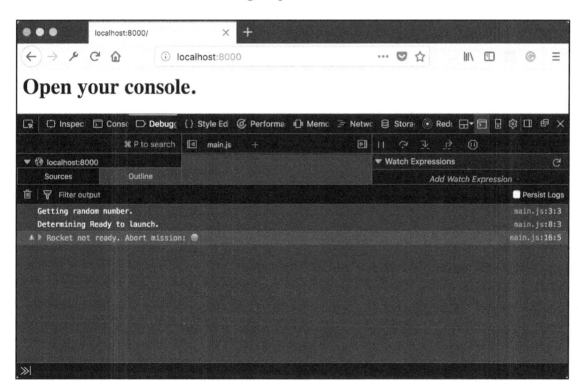

How it works...

Because our `main` function is marked as `async`, we are able to use the `await` operator in its body. This operator causes the function to wait for the result of the expression to be resolved. In our case, this means the Promise created by the `async` function we called is fulfilled.

Once the result is fulfilled, the control flow continues to the next statement. If we did not use the `await` operator, the value of `randomNumber` would be a promise that would resolve to the returned value. We could handle this with the promise interface, but because we used `await` , we are able to write something that looks more like synchronous code.

See also

- *Awaiting multiple results concurrently*

Awaiting multiple results concurrently

Sometimes it's possible to initiate multiple asynchronous operations at the same time. This can be desirable, for example, if multiple network requests are necessary in order to fetch all the data for a given page. Waiting for each request to finish before starting the next one wastes time.

In this recipe, we'll see how to use `await` to initiate and wait for multiple results concurrently.

Getting ready

This recipe assumes you already have a workspace that allows you to create and run ES modules in your browser. If you don't, please see the first two chapters.

How to do it...

1. Open your command-line application and navigate to your workspace.
2. Create a new folder named `04-05-await-concurrently`.
3. Create three functions, `checkEngines`, `checkFlightPlan`, and `checkNavigationSystem` that log a message when they start and return a `Promise` that resolves to `true` if a random number is higher than a threshold after some timeout:

```
function checkEngines() {
  console.log('checking engine');

  return new Promise(function (resolve) {
    setTimeout(function () {
      console.log('engine check completed');
      resolve(Math.random() < 0.9)
    }, 250)
  });
}

function checkFlightPlan() {
  console.log('checking flight plan');

  return new Promise(function (resolve) {
    setTimeout(function () {
      console.log('flight plan check completed');
      resolve(Math.random() < 0.9)
    }, 350)
  });
}

function checkNavigationSystem() {
  console.log('checking navigation system');

  return new Promise(function (resolve) {
    setTimeout(function () {
      console.log('navigation system check completed');
      resolve(Math.random() < 0.9)
    }, 450)
  });
}
```

4. Create an `async` as the `main` function that calls each of the functions created in the previous step. Assign the returned value from each to a local variable. Then await the result of the Promise, and log out the results:

```
export async function main() {
  const enginePromise = checkEngines();
  const flighPlanPromise = checkFlightPlan(0.5);
  const navSystemPromise = checkNavigationSystem(0.75);
  const enginesOk = await enginePromise;
  const flighPlanOk = await flighPlanPromise;
  const navigationOk = await navSystemPromise;

  if (enginesOk && flighPlanOk && navigationOk) {
    console.log('All systems go, ready to launch: 🚀');
  } else {
    console.error('Abort the launch: ⚫');
    if (!enginesOk) {
      console.error('engines not ready');
    }
    if (flighPlanOk) {
      console.error('error found in flight plan');
    }

    if (navigationOk) {
      console.error('error found in navigation systems');
    }
  }
}
```

5. Start your Python web server and open the following link in your browser: `http://localhost:8000/`.

6. You should see the following output:

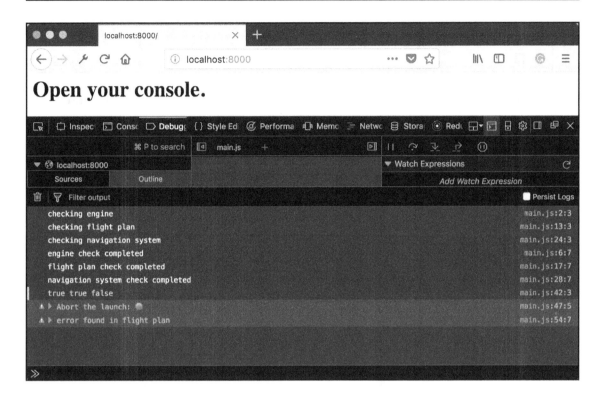

How it works...

You'll see in the output that the `checking` messages are logged immediately. Because all of the functions are called before the first `await` usage, the operations are initiated right await. This allows all the timeouts to start before any have completed.

Once `await` is used, the `main` function will block until the result is resolved. The code synchronizes again. The results of each function are resolved in sequence, but the long-running portions of the code (`setTimeout`) are concurrent.

The three check functions had to return Promises manually, because we are using `setTimeout`. Because this function uses a callback, we can't use `async/await`.

Using Promise.all to collect an array of async results

In the previous recipe, we saw how to trigger multiple asynchronous functions before awaiting their results. We've also seen how well the Promise API and `asyc/await` operators work together. There are some situations where it is preferable to use the Promise API.

In this recipe, we'll see how to use `Promise.all` to collect the result of multiple asynchronous operations.

Getting ready

This recipe assumes you already have a workspace that allows you to create and run ES modules in your browser. If you don't, please see the first two chapters.

How to do it...

1. Open your command-line application and navigate to your workspace.
2. Create a new folder named `04-06-Promise-all-collect-concurrently`.
3. Create three functions, `checkEngines`, `checkFlightPlan`, and `checkNavigationSystem` that log a message when they start and return a `Promise` that resolves to `true` if a random number is higher than a threshold after some timeout:

```
function checkEngines() {
  console.log('checking engine');

  return new Promise(function (resolve) {
    setTimeout(function() {
      console.log('engine check completed');
      resolve(Math.random() < 0.9)
    }, 250)
  });
}

function checkFlightPlan() {
  console.log('checking flight plan');
```

```
      return new Promise(function (resolve) {
        setTimeout(function() {
          console.log('flight plan check completed');
          resolve(Math.random() < 0.9)
        }, 350)
      });
    }

    function checkNavigationSystem() {
      console.log('checking navigation system');

      return new Promise(function (resolve) {
        setTimeout(function() {
          console.log('navigation system check completed');
          resolve(Math.random() < 0.9)
        }, 450)
      });
    }
```

4. Create an `async` as the `main` function that calls each of the functions created in the previous step. Collect the results with `Promise.all`, reduce the results into a single ok to launch value, and log the result:

```
export async function main() {
  const prelaunchChecks = [
    checkEngines(),
    checkFlightPlan(0.5),
    checkNavigationSystem(0.75)
  ];

  const checkResults = await Promise.all(prelaunchChecks);
  const readyToLaunch = checkResults.reduce((acc, curr) => acc
&&
  curr);

  if (readyToLaunch) {
    console.log('All systems go, ready to launch: 🚀');
  } else {
    console.error('Something went wrong, abort the launch: ⬤
');
  }
}
```

5. Start your Python web server and open the following link in your browser: `http://localhost:8000/`.

6. You should see the following output:

How it works...

`Promise.all` returns a Promise that resolves to an array of values resolved from multiple values. In our case, those are the asynchronous functions we created in *Step 3*. Once that Promise is created, we can await the result.

Once we have this result, we can use the `Array.prototype.reduce` method in order to create a single Boolean value that can be used in a conditional.

If we compare this recipe to the prior recipe, we can see an advantage. Adding another pre-launch check is as simple as adding another asynchronous function to the array of functions. In fact, we don't need to know ahead of time how may pre-launch checks have to be performed. If they all resolve to a Boolean value, they will work with `Promise.all`. We lose information about which step failed, but we'll see in future recipes how to regain this information with error handling.

There's more...

It's possible to refactor the `main` function so that the pre-check functions are executed implicitly. We can use the `Array.prototype.map` function to do this:

```
export async function main() {
 const prelaunchChecks = [
   checkEngines,
   checkFlightPlan,
   checkNavigationSystem
 ];
 const checkResults = await Promise.all(prelaunchChecks.map((check) =>
 check());
 const readyToLaunch = checkResults.reduce((acc, curr) => acc &&
 curr);

 if (readyToLaunch) {
   console.log('All systems go, ready to launch: 🚀');
 } else {
   console.error('Something went wrong, abort the launch: ⚫');
 }
```

The highlighted section shows that the asynchronous functions are called within a map.

See also

- Using `Array.reduce` to transform data
- *Handling errors thrown inside of* `Promise.all`

Handling errors when awaiting an async function

So far in this chapter, we've seen how to work with `async` functions that fulfill successfully. But, as we know, this is not always the case. We need to be able to handle errors that are thrown by asynchronous functions, or any functions they call.

In this recipe, we'll see how `try-catch` blocks can handle errors that are thrown by `async` functions.

Getting ready

This recipe assumes you already have a workspace that allows you to create and run ES modules in your browser. If you don't, please see the first two chapters.

How to do it...

1. Open your command-line application and navigate to your workspace.
2. Create a new folder named 4-07- async-errors-try-catch.
3. Copy or create an index.html that loads and runs a main function from main.js.
4. Create an async function, addBoosters, that throws some error:

```
async function addBoosters() {
  throw new Error('Unable to add Boosters');
}
```

5. Create an async function, performGuidanceDiagnostic, that also throws an error:

```
async function performGuidanceDiagnostic (rocket) {
  throw new Error('Unable to finish guidance diagnostic'));
}
```

6. Create an async as the main function that calls addBosters and performGuidanceDiagnostic and handles the error:

```
export async function main() {
  console.log('Before Check');

  try {
    await addBosters();
    await performGuidanceDiagnostic();
  } catch (e) {
    console.error(e);
  }
}

  console.log('After Check');
```

7. Start your Python web server and open the following link in your browser: http://localhost:8000/.

8. You should see the following output:

How it works...

When we `await` a result from an asynchronous function that fulfills with an error state, an error is thrown. To continue with the program, we need to catch this error. In the preceding recipe, the first asynchronous function throws so the second operation isn't performed, then we log the error to the console before exiting the `try-catch` block.

This compares favorably with Promise chain error handling, which uses the same `try-catch` mechanism for error handling as synchronous code. We don't need to wrap synchronous code with promises so that they can work with `Promise.catch`; we can use the language level `try-catch` blocks.

In the next recipe, we'll see how `try-catch` works with multiple asynchronous operations operating concurrently.

Handling errors thrown inside of Promise.all

In a prior recipe, we saw how to use `Promise.all` to collect the results of multiple asynchronous functions. In an error state, `Promise.all` is even more interesting. Often, when dealing with multiple possible error conditions, we have to write a log of Boolean logic if we want to display multiple error messages. But, in this recipe, we'll see how we can use `Promise.all` and `try-catch` blocks to handle multiple error conditions concurrently, without complicated Boolean logic.

Getting ready

This recipe assumes you already have a workspace that allows you to create and run ES modules in your browser. If you don't, please see the first two chapters.

How to do it...

1. Open your command-line application and navigate to your workspace.
2. Create a new folder named `04-06-Promise-all-collect-concurrently`.
3. Create three `async` functions, `checkEngines`, `checkFlightPlan`, and `checkNavigationSystem` that log a message when they start and return a `Promise` that rejects an error if a random number is higher than a threshold or resolve, after some timeout:

```
function checkEngines() {
  console.log('checking engine');

  return new Promise(function (resolve, reject) {
    setTimeout(function () {
      if (Math.random() > 0.5) {
        reject(new Error('Engine check failed'));
      } else {
        console.log('Engine check completed');
        resolve();
      }
    }, 250)
  });
}


function checkFlightPlan() {
```

```
console.log('checking flight plan');

return new Promise(function (resolve, reject) {
  setTimeout(function () {
    if (Math.random() > 0.5) {
      reject(new Error('Flight plan check failed'));
    } else {
      console.log('Flight plan check completed');
      resolve();
    }
  }, 350)
});
}


function checkNavigationSystem() {
  console.log('checking navigation system');

  return new Promise(function (resolve, reject) {
    setTimeout(function () {
      if (Math.random() > 0.5) {
        reject(new Error('Navigation system check failed'));
      } else {
        console.log('Navigation system check completed');
        resolve();
      }
    }, 450)
  });
}
```

4. Create an `async` as the `main` function that calls each of the functions created in the previous step. Await the results, and catch and log any errors that are thrown. Log success if no error is thrown:

```
export async function main() {
  try {
    const prelaunchChecks = [
      checkEngines,
      checkFlightPlan,
      checkNavigationSystem
    ];
    await Promise.all(prelauchCheck.map((check) => check());
;

    console.log('All systems go, ready to launch: 🚀');
  } catch (e) {
    console.error('Aborting launch: ⬤');
```

```
                console.error(e);
            }
        }
```

5. Start your Python web server and open the following link in your browser:
    `http://localhost:8000/`.

6. You should see the following output:

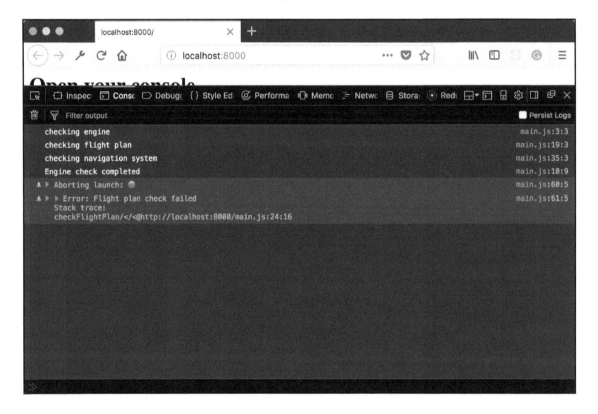

How it works...

As we have seen before, `Promise.all` returns a Promise that resolves to an array of values resolved from multiple values, and we can `await` those values when they are fulfilled. When we `await` a Promise that is resolved in an error state, an exception is thrown.

What is interesting about the preceding code is that three asynchronous promises are executing concurrently. If one or more of them is fulfilled with an error, then one or more errors will be thrown.

You'll notice that only one error is ever caught and logged. As with synchronous code, we may potentially have multiple errors thrown by our code, but only one will be caught and logged by the `catch` block.

Using finally to ensure an operation is performed

Error handling can get fairly complicated. There may be cases where you want to allow an error to continue bubbling up the call stack to be handled at a higher level. In those cases, you may also need to perform some cleanup tasks. Often this can mean resetting some shared resource, but it could also simply be logging the current state of the application.

In this recipe, we'll see how to use `finally` to ensure that some code is executed, regardless of the error state.

Getting ready

This recipe assumes you already have a workspace that allows you to create and run ES modules in your browser. If you don't, please see the first two chapters.

How to do it...

1. Open your command-line application and navigate to your workspace.
2. Create a new folder named `04-06-Promise-all-collect-concurrently`.
3. Create three `async` functions, `checkEngines`, `checkFlightPlan`, and `checkNavigationSystem` that log a message when they start and return a `Promise` that rejects an error if a random number is higher than a threshold, or resolve after some timeout:

```
function checkEngines() {
  console.log('checking engine');

  return new Promise(function (resolve, reject) {
    setTimeout(function () {
      if (Math.random() > 0.5) {
        reject(new Error('Engine check failed'));
      } else {
```

```
                console.log('Engine check completed');
                resolve();
            }
        }, 250)
    });
}


function checkFlightPlan() {
  console.log('checking flight plan');

  return new Promise(function (resolve, reject) {
    setTimeout(function () {
      if (Math.random() > 0.5) {
        reject(new Error('Flight plan check failed'));
      } else {
        console.log('Flight plan check completed');
        resolve();
      }
    }, 350)
  });
}


function checkNavigationSystem() {
  console.log('checking navigation system');

  return new Promise(function (resolve, reject) {
    setTimeout(function () {
      if (Math.random() > 0.5) {
        reject(new Error('Navigation system check failed'));
      } else {
        console.log('Navigation system check completed');
        resolve();
      }
    }, 450)
  });
}
```

4. Create an `asyncperformCheck` function that calls each of the functions created in the previous step. Await the results, and use `finally` to log a complete message:

```
async function performChecks() {
  console.log('Starting Pre-Launch Checks');
  try {
    const prelaunchChecks = [
      checkEngines,
      checkFlightPlan,
      checkNavigationSystem
    ];

    return Promise.all(prelauchCheck.map((check) => check()));

  } finally {
    console.log('Completed Pre-Launch Checks');
  }
}
```

5. Create an `async` as the `main` function that calls the `performCheck` function. Await the results, use `try-catch` to handle any errors, and log out whether the launch can continue or not:

```
export async function main() {
  try {
    await performChecks();
    console.log('All systems go, ready to launch: 🚀');
  } catch (e) {
    console.error('Aborting launch: 🌑');
    console.error(e);
  }
}
```

6. Start your Python web server and open the following link in your browser: `http://localhost:8000/`.

7. You should see the following output:

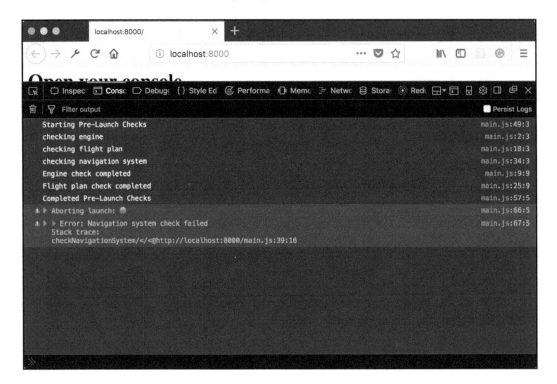

How it works...

As in the preceding recipe, the errors are caught by the `main` function, and the launch continue or abort message is displayed. In this recipe, we've grouped the `check` function into a single asynchronous function, `performChecks`, that lets us know when they have all finished.

Because `performChecks` does not have a `catch` block on the awaited Promise result, the errors thrown lower in the call stack bubble up to the `main` function. However, the `finally` block ensures that there is a message to let us know that the `performChecks` has completed.

You can imagine that this organization could be expanded to include multiple layers, and other branches of operations. Handling errors is an important task in large programs, and `async/await` allows us to use the `try-catch` blocks to handle errors from asynchronous and synchronous code in the same way.

Web Workers, Shared Memory, and Atomics

5

In this chapter, we will cover the following recipes:

- Performing work on separate threads with Web Workers
- Sending messages to and from Web Workers
- Sending data to Web Workers
- Stopping workers with terminate
- Creating SharedArrayBuffer
- Sending SharedArrayBuffer to a Web Worker
- Reading SharedArray from multiple Web Workers
- Using Atomics to coordinate use of shared memory
- Using promises to provide a simple interface for a worker

Introduction

The capabilities and expectations of JavaScript and web applications are expanding every day. One of the most exciting areas this expansion has led to is parallel programming, which is related to, but not synonymous with, asynchronous and concurrent programming. Parallel programming allows for multiple operations to take place simultaneously rather than interleaving them.

This distinction may seem small, but it is quite significant. In this chapter, we will see how to use the facilities available on the web platform to create programs that execute in parallel. Web Workers will be used to create parallel jobs, `SharedMemoryBuffer` to share information, and the Atomic API to coordinate between them.

Enabling SharedArrayBuffers in Firefox

In early 2018, the Spectre and Meltdown vulnerabilities were discovered. In response, browser manufacturers disabled `SharedArrayBuffer` by default. Some of the recipes in this chapter require this feature. This recipe demonstrates how to enable them in Firefox.

Getting ready

This recipe assumes that you have an up to date version of Firefox installed.

How to do it...

1. Open Firefox.
2. Navigate to `about:config`.
3. Click **I accept the risk!**
4. Search for **shared**.
5. Double-click **javascript.options.shared_memory**.
6. This option should now have the value **true**:

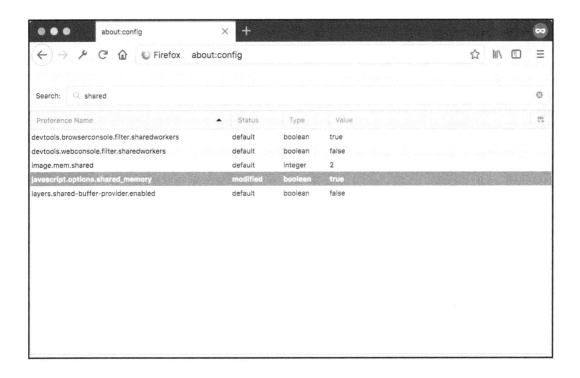

How it works...

By default, shared memory is disabled in Firefox, but the options let developers activate these (potentially insecure) features without exposing normal users to them. You can read more about Meltdown and Spectre at:

`https://meltdownattack.com/`.

You should not leave this feature enabled after you finish experimenting with it.

Enabling SharedArrayBuffers in Chrome

In early 2018, the Spectre and Meltdown vulnerabilities were discovered. In response, browser manufacturers disabled `SharedArrayBuffer` by default. Some of the recipes in this chapter require this feature. This recipe demonstrates how to enable them in Chrome.

Getting ready

This recipe assumes that you have an up to date version of Chrome installed.

How to do it...

1. Open Chrome.
2. Navigate to `chrome://flags/`.
3. Click **I accept the risk!**
4. Search for **shared**.
5. Select **Enabled** for the option **Experimental enabled SharedArrayBuffer support in JavaScript.**
6. Click **RELAUNCH NOW**:

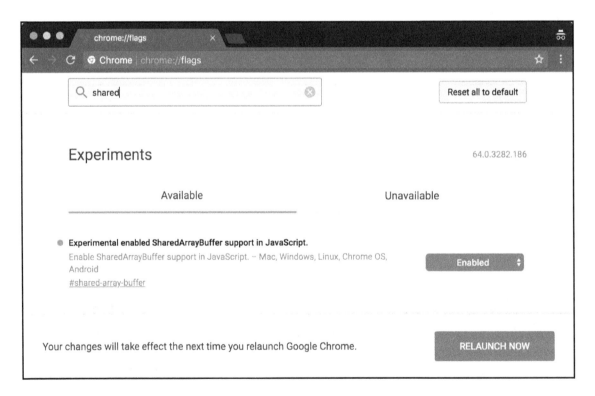

How it works...

By default, shared memory is disabled in Firefox, but the options let developers activate these (potentially insecure) features without exposing normal users to them. You can read more about Meltdown and Spectre at:
https://meltdownattack.com/.

You should not leave this feature enabled after you finish experimenting with it.

Performing work on separate threads with Web Workers

Web Workers allow browser operations to take place outside the main thread. Once created, communication between threads is made by passing messages. In this recipe, we'll see how to create a very simple worker, and send it a message from the main thread.

Getting ready

This recipe assumes that you already have a workspace that allows you to create and run ES modules in your browser. If you don't, please see the first two chapters.

How to do it...

1. Open your command-line application and navigate to your workspace.
2. Create a new folder named `05-01-performing-work-with-web-workers`.
3. Copy or create an `index.html` that loads and runs a `main` function from `main.js`.
4. Create a `main.js` file with a `main` function that creates a worker from a file named `worker.js`. Then post a message of type `hello-message` to the `worker`:

```
// main.js
export function main() {
  console.log('Hello, from main.');
  const worker = new Worker('./worker.js');
  worker.postMessage({ type: 'hello-message' });
}
```

5. Create a file named `worker.js` that logs a `Hello` message:

```
// worker.js
console.log('Hello, from the worker.');
```

6. In the `worker.js` file, set the `onmessage` callback on the global scope. This function should log out the type of the message received:

```
// worker.js
console.log('Hello, from the worker.');

this.onmessage = function (message) {
    console.log('Message Recieved: (%s)', message.data.type);
}
```

7. Start your Python web server and open the following link in your browser: `http://localhost:8000/`.

8. You should see the following output displayed:

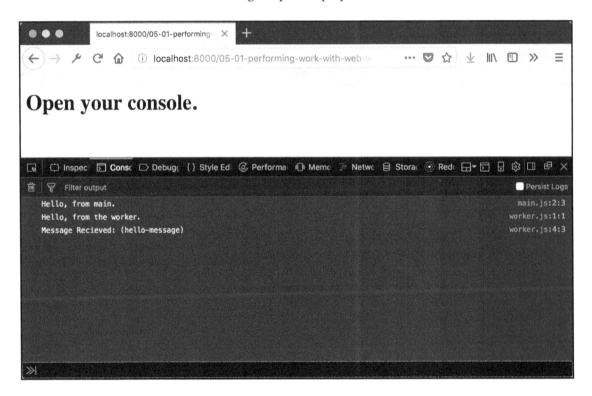

How it works...

Constructing the worker with the name of the worker file creates a worker on a new thread. By setting the `onmessage` event listener on the global context of the worker, we are able to receive messages from the main thread.

After creating the worker, the `main` function can use that reference to post messages to the new worker. The argument of the `postMessage` method is passed to the worker as the `data` attribute of the `message` property that is received.

Sending messages to and from Web Workers

In the previous recipe, we saw how to create and send a message to a worker on a background thread. That's pretty great! Before Web Workers were introduced, it wasn't possible for JavaScript to work with anything but the main thread. However, it isn't very useful if we can't get any information back.

In this recipe, we'll see how to wait for, and send responses back from, a Web Worker.

Getting ready

This recipe assumes you already have a workspace that allows you to create and run ES modules in your browser. If you don't, please see the first two chapters.

How to do it...

1. Open your command-line application and navigate to your workspace.
2. Create a new folder named `05-02-send-messages-to-and-from-web-workers`.
3. Copy or create an `index.html` that loads and runs a `main` function from `main.js`.

4. Create a `main.js` with a function named `onMessage` that takes an argument `message` and logs out the `type` and `index` properties:

```
// main.js
function onMessage(message) {
  const { type, index } = message.data;
  console.log('Main recieved a messge (%s) from index: (%s)',
           type, index);
}
```

5. Set a `WORKER_COUNT` constant:

```
// main.js
const WORKER_COUNT = 5;
```

6. Create a `main` function that creates `WORKER_COUNT` workers, sets the `onMessage` property, and posts the `index` to the worker:

```
export function main() {
  for (let index = 0; index < WORKER_COUNT; index++) {
    const worker = new Worker('./worker.js');

    worker.onmessage = onMessage;
    worker.postMessage({ type: 'ping', index });
  }
}
```

7. Create a `worker.js` file that assigns the current context as a `global` constant:

```
// worker.js
const global = this;
```

8. Set the `onmessage` event listener on `global` to the global context. The function should take a message argument and log out the `index` and `type` properties. Then it should call `global.postMessage` with another message, passing back its `index`:

```
// worker.js
global.onmessage = (message) => {
  const { type, index } = message.data;
  console.log('Worker (%s) recieved a messge (%s)', index,
type);

  global.postMessage({ index, type: 'pong' })
  global.postMessage({ index, type: 'another-type' })
};
```

9. Start your Python web server and open the following link in your browser: `http://localhost:8000/`.

10. You should see the following output displayed:

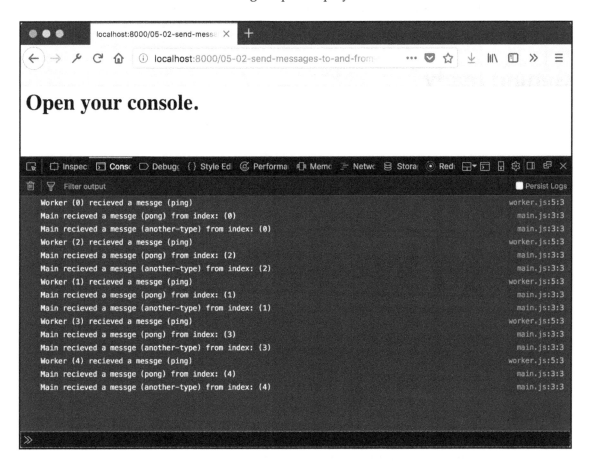

How it works...

We've seen how the `onmessage` listener can be used to listen for messages posted from the main thread. Now we can see that the same evenlistener, when binding on the worker reference in the `main` function, can listen to messages from the worker. We also can see that this listener is isolated from the individual worker being referenced. Each worker has a unique event listener; this is useful for organizing communication between workers.

Sending data to a Web Worker

Now that we've seen how to send messages back and forth, we can start to actually put these Web Workers to work. In this recipe, we'll see that you can send data to and from a Web Worker.

Getting ready

This recipe assumes you already have a workspace that allows you to create and run ES modules in your browser. If you don't, please see the first two chapters.

How to do it...

1. Open your command-line application and navigate to your workspace.
2. Create a new folder named `05-03-send-data-to-and-from-web-workers`.
3. Copy or create an `index.html` that loads and runs a `main` function from `main.js`.
4. Create a `main.js` with a function named `onMessage` that takes an argument `message` and logs out the `type` and `index` properties:

```
// main.js
function onMessage(message) {
  const { result, type } = message.data;
  console.log('Result for operation (%s): (%s)', type, result);
}
```

5. Create a `main` function that creates a worker, sets the `onMessage` property, creates an array of random numbers, and posts two messages to the worker, one to sum some of the numbers and another to average them:

```
export function main() {
  const worker = new Worker('./worker.js');
  worker.onmessage = onMessage;

  const numbers = (new Array(100)).fill().map(Math.random)
  worker.postMessage({ type: 'average', numbers});
}
```

6. Create a `worker.js` file that assigns the current context as a `global` constant:

```
// worker.js
const global = this;
```

7. Set the `onmessage` event listener on `global` to the context. The function should take a message argument and perform either a sum or average operation on the numbers property of `message.data`:

```
// worker.js
global.onmessage = (message) => {
  const { type, numbers } = message.data;

  switch (type) {
    case 'sum':
      const sum = numbers.reduce((acc, curr) => acc + curr, 0);
      global.postMessage({ result: sum, type })
      break;
    case 'average':
      const average = numbers.reduce((acc, curr) => acc + curr,
       0) /numbers.length;
      global.postMessage({ result: average, type })
      break;
  }
};
```

8. Start your Python web server and open the following link in your browser: `http://localhost:8000/`.

9. You should see the following output:

How it works...

We've seen a simple string posted to and from workers. Now we can see that more complex objects can be sent as well. In fact, a sizable number of types can be passed via `postMessage`.

 To see a full list of valid types, visit the link:
`https://developer.mozilla.org/en-US/docs/Web/API/Web_Workers_API/Structured_clone_algorithm`.

By using `postMessage`, we have copied the data to the worker. This operation is costly, because whenever the message is posted to a new thread, the data must be duplicated in order to be available. For small datasets, this isn't a problem, but for larger sets it can be slow and memory-intensive. For future recipes in this chapter, we'll be using shared memory to avoid this copying.

Stopping workers with terminate

Not all problems are cumulative. Some have a desired goal state; once it is found, then the program can exit. We've seen that workers communicate their results by posting messages. Now our program is completed, it would be nice to prevent future messages from being received, possibly polluting our results.

In this recipe, we'll see how to use `Worker.terminate` to immediately stop a `Worker`.

Getting ready

This recipe assumes you already have a workspace that allows you to create and run ES modules in your browser. If you don't, please see the first two chapters.

How to do it...

1. Open your command-line application and navigate to your workspace.
2. Create a new folder named `05-04-stop-workers-with-terminate`.
3. Copy or create an `index.html` that loads and runs a `main` function from `main.js`.

4. Create a `main.js` with a function named `onMessage` that takes a `message` and `workers` argument, logs out the `type` and `timeout` properties of `message.data`, and calls `terminate` on all the `workers`:

```
// main.js
function onComplete(message, workers) {
  const { index, timeout } = message.data;
  workers.map((w) => w.terminate());

  console.log(
    'Result from worker (%s) after timeout (%s): %s',
    index,
    timeout
  );
}
```

5. Create a `main` function that creates multiple workers, sets the `onMessage` property with a function that passes all the `workers` as the second argument, then posts a message to each with the `index`:

```
export function main() {
const totalWorkers = 10;
const workers = [];

for (let i = 0; i < totalWorkers; i++) {
  const worker = new Worker('./worker.js');
  worker.onmessage = (msg) => onComplete(msg, workers);
  workers.push(worker);
}

workers.map((worker, index) => {
  workers[index].postMessage({ index });
});
}
```

6. Create a `worker.js` file that assigns the current context as a `global` constant:

```
// worker.js
const global = this;
```

7. Set a `timeout` constant to some random number between *0* and *10,000*:

```
// worker.js
const timeout = Math.floor(Math.random() * 10000);
```

8. Set the `onmessage` event listener on `global` to the context. The function should take a `message` argument and post a response message with the `index` and `timeout` of this worker, after the given timeout:

```
// worker.js
global.onmessage = (message) => {
  const data = JSON.parse(message.data);
  const data = {
    index: data.index,
    timeout: timeout
  };

  setTimeout(() => global.postMessage(data), timeout)
};
```

9. Start your Python web server and open the following link in your browser: `http://localhost:8000/`.

10. You should see the following output displayed:

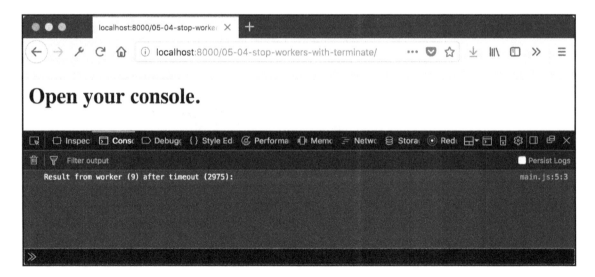

How it works...

All 10 workers are instructed to post a message after their given timeout but, as you can see, only a single worker actually posts a message back to the main thread. This is because, after this first worker posts, we call `terminate` on all of the workers. This means that they will stop immediately, and unless another worker has already posted, it never will. So, we will almost always see a single message posted. It is possible that one or two other workers will post before being terminated.

Creating SharedArrayBuffer

So far, we've see how to send data between the main thread and workers. The downside of how we've done this so far is that the data is copied. This means that as the amount of data and number of workers increase, so does the amount of copying that has to be done. Luckily, there is a way to share data between threads with less overhead.

`SharedArrayBuffer` can be shared between arrays without copying data. In this recipe, we'll see how to create, as well as read and write, data from a `SharedArrayBuffer`.

Getting ready

This recipe assumes you already have a workspace that allows you to create and run ES modules in your browser. If you don't, please see the first two chapters.

How to do it...

1. Open your command-line application, and navigate to your workspace.
2. Create a new folder named `05-05-creating-shared-array-buffer`.
3. Copy or create an `index.html` that loads and runs a `main` function from `main.js`.

4. Create a `main.js` file with a main method that defines constants for `NUM_COUNT`, `BYTES_FOR_32_BIT`, `ARRAY_SIZE`, and `MAX_NUMBER`:

```
export function main() {
  const NUM_COUNT = 2048;
  const BYTES_FOR_32_BIT = 4;
  const ARRAY_SIZE = NUM_COUNT * BYTES_FOR_32_BIT;
  const MAX_NUMBER = 1024;
}
```

5. Next, create a `SharedArrayBuffer` that is of size `ARRAY_SIZE`, and create an `Int32Array` casting of it:

```
export function main() {
  // ...
  const sab = new SharedArrayBuffer(ARRAY_SIZE);
  const intBuffer = new Int32Array(sab);
}
```

6. Fill the `intBuffer` with random numbers between *0* and `MAX_NUMBER`:

```
export function main() {
  // ...
  // fill with random numbers  // fill with random numbers
  intBuffer.forEach((value, index) => {
    intBuffer[index] = Math.random() * MAX_NUMBER;
  });
}
```

7. Calculate and print the sum of the values in the array:

```
export function main() {
  // ...
  // sum the ints
  const sum = intBuffer.reduce((acc, number) =>
    acc + number
  , 0);
}
```

8. Start your Python web server and open the following link in your browser: `http://localhost:8000/`.

9. You should see the following output:

How it works...

It feels a little unnatural to be thinking about byte size when working in JavaScript, but it's necessary for working with `SharedArrayBuffer`. The preceding example creates an array of 2,048 32-bit integers. So in order to create a `SharedArray` buffer we have to calculate how much memory 2,048 32-bit integers will take up. This is done with simple multiplication. Once we have `ARRAY_SIZE` we can allocate the memory.

Now that we have the array, we need to cast it as some type in order to read and write from it. We're using `Int32Array`, so when we perform array access operations the values will be cast as 32-bit integers.

When filling the array, we simply loop over each number and multiply a random number by the `MAX_NUMBER`; the resulting value is cast as a 32-bit integer (the decimal value is lost). Next, summing is done with the array's `reduce` function, and we log out the results.

A nice feature of the `Int32Array` is that it has all of the Array methods as well. So we can perform map, join, index, includes, and so on with the new data type.

Sending SharedArrayBuffer to a Web Worker

Now that we know how to create and use a `SharedArrayBuffer`, we can use one to share data between the main thread and workers. As mentioned previously, this has an advantage over posting JavaScript objects, in that the data doesn't need to be copied; it is shared.

In this recipe, we'll see how to share a `SharedArrayBuffer` with a worker, and post the result back to the main thread.

Getting ready

This recipe assumes you already have a workspace that allows you to create and run ES modules in your browser. If you don't, please see the first two chapters. It also assumes that you have enabled shared memory in your browser. If you haven't please see the recipes at the beginning of this chapter.

How to do it...

1. Open your command-line application, and navigate to your workspace.
2. Create a new folder named `05-06-sending-shared-array-to-worker`.
3. Copy or create an `index.html` that loads and runs a `main` function from `main.js`.
4. Create a `main.js` file with an `onMessage` function that logs out the `result` and `type` members of the received message data:

```
function onMessage(message) {
  const { result, type } = message.data;
  console.log('result from worker operation: %s', type,
result);
}
```

5. Create a `main.js` file with a main method that defines constants for NUM_COUNT, BYTES_FOR_32_BIT, ARRAY_SIZE, and MAX_NUMBER:

```
export function main() {
  const NUM_COUNT = 2048;
  const BYTES_FOR_32_BIT = 4;
  const ARRAY_SIZE = NUM_COUNT * BYTES_FOR_32_BIT;
  const MAX_NUMBER = 1024;
}
```

6. Next, create a `SharedArrayBuffer` that is of size ARRAY_SIZE, and create a worker with the source in `worker.js`:

```
export function main() {
  // ...
  const sab = new SharedArrayBuffer(ARRAY_SIZE);
  const worker = new Worker('./worker.js');
}
```

7. Set the worker on the message event listener to the `onMessage` function, and post a message to the worker with the array buffer:

```
export function main() {
  // ...
  worker.onmessage = onMessage;
  worker.postMessage({ type: 'load-array', array: sab });;
}
```

8. Fill the array buffer with 32-bit integers with random values between 0 and MAX_NUMBER:

```
export function main() {
  // ...
  const intBuffer = new Int32Array(sab);
  // fill with random numbers
  intBuffer.forEach((value, index) => {
    intBuffer[index] = Math.random() * MAX_NUMBER;
  });
}
```

9. Post messages to the worker, requesting calculations of sum and average:

```
export function main() {
  // ...
  worker.postMessage({ type: 'calculate-sum' });
  worker.postMessage({ type: 'calculate-average'});
}
```

10. Create a worker.js file, assign the current context to a variable global, declare a variable named sharedIntArray, and assign a function to the onmessage event:

```
// worker.js
const global = this;
let sharedIntArray;

global.onmessage = (message) => {};
```

11. In the onmessage listener get the data component of the message argument, and switch on the type attribute:

```
global.onmessage = (message) => {
  const { data } = message;
  switch (data.type) {}
};
```

12. Add a case for 'load-array', where we assign the array property of data to sharedIntArray after casting it as an Int32Array:

```
global.onmessage = (message) => {
  const { data } = message;
  switch (data.type) {
    case 'load-array':
      sharedIntArray = new Int32Array(data.array);
      break;
  }
};
```

13. Add a case for `'calculate-sum'` that sums all the numbers in the array and posts the result back to the main thread:

```
global.onmessage = (message) => {
  const { data } = message;
  switch (data.type) {
    case 'load-array':
      sharedIntArray = new Int32Array(data.array);
      break;
    case 'calculate-sum':
      const sum = sharedIntArray.reduce((acc, number) => acc +
      number,
      0);
      global.postMessage({ type: 'sum', result: sum });
      break;
  }
};
```

14. Add a case for `'calculate-average'` that averages all the numbers in the array and posts the result back to the main thread:

```
global.onmessage = (message) => {
  const { data } = message;
  switch (data.type) {
    case 'load-array':
      sharedIntArray = new Int32Array(data.array);
      break;
    case 'calculate-sum':
      const sum = sharedIntArray.reduce((acc, number) =>
        acc + number,
      0);
      global.postMessage({ type: 'sum', result: sum });
      break;

    case 'calculate-average':
      const total = sharedIntArray.reduce((acc, number) =>
        acc + number
      , 0);
      const average = total / sharedIntArray.length;
      global.postMessage({ type: 'average', result: average });
      break;
  }
};
```

15. Start your Python web server and open the following link in your browser: http://localhost:8000/.

16. You should see the following output:

How it works...

As mentioned previously, `SharedArrayBuffer` is not copied between threads. It is shared. So, when we create the shared array buffer and pass that reference to a worker, the values inserted into the array by the main thread are available in the worker.

After the worker receives messages to perform calculations, the values can be accumulated as they were in any other array, and the value sent back is a simple message.

Reading SharedArray from multiple Web Workers

In the previous recipe, we saw how data can be shared between the main thread and a single worker. This is helpful for move long-running operations on the main thread, which helps keep the UI responsive. However, it isn't taking full advantage of parallel processing. With very large datasets, breaking up the computation between many workers can be advantageous.

In this recipe, we'll see how to use multiple workers to produce portions of a result.

Getting ready

This recipe assumes you already have a workspace that allows you to create and run ES modules in your browser. If you don't, please see the first two chapters.

How to do it...

1. Open your command-line application and navigate to your workspace.
2. Create a new folder named `05-07-reading-shared-buffer-from-multiple-workers`.
3. Copy or create an `index.html` that loads and runs a `main` function from `main.js`.
4. Create a `main.js` file with an `onMessage` function that logs out the following members of the message data: `workenIndex`, `type`, `result`, `workerIndex`, `startIndex`, `endIndex`, and `windowSize`:

```js
// main.js
function onMessage(message) {
const {
    type,
    result,
    workerIndex,
    startIndex,
    endIndex,
    windowSize
} = message.data;
console.log(`Result from worker operation {
    type: ${type},
    result: ${result},
    workerIndex: ${workerIndex},
    startIndex: ${startIndex},
    endIndex: ${endIndex},
    windowSize: ${windowSize}
}`);
}
```

5. Create a `main.js` file with a main method that defines constants for `NUM_COUNT`, `BYTES_FOR_32_BIT`, `ARRAY_SIZE`, `WORKER_COUNT`, and `MAX_NUMBER`:

```
export function main() {
  console.log('Main function starting.');
  const NUM_COUNT = 2048;
  const BYTES_FOR_32_BIT = 4;
  const ARRAY_SIZE = NUM_COUNT * BYTES_FOR_32_BIT;
  const MAX_NUMBER = 32;
  const WORKER_COUNT = 10;
}
```

6. Next, create an array of workers of size `WORKER_COUNT`:

```
export function main() {
  // ...
  // create workers
  let workers = [];
  console.log('Creating workers.');
  for (let i = 0; i < WORKER_COUNT; i++) {
    const worker = new Worker('./worker.js');
    worker.onmessage = onMessage;
    workers = workers.concat(worker);
  }
}
```

7. Next, create a `SharedArrayBuffer` that is of size `ARRAY_SIZE`, and fill it with random integers:

```
export function main() {
  // ...
  // create buffer and add data
  const sab = new SharedArrayBuffer(ARRAY_SIZE);
  const intBuffer = new Int32Array(sab);
  // fill with random numbers
  console.log('Filling Int buffer');
  intBuffer.forEach((value, index) => {
    intBuffer[index] = (Math.random() * MAX_NUMBER) + 1;
  });
}
```

8. Post these messages to each of the workers: `'load-array'`, `'load-indices'`, `'calculate-sum'`, and `'calculate-average'`:

```
export function main() {
    // ...
    workers.forEach((worker, workerIndex) => {
        worker.postMessage({ type: 'load-array', array: sab });
        worker.postMessage({ type: 'load-indices', workerIndex,
        workerCount: WORKER_COUNT });
        worker.postMessage({ type: 'calculate-sum' });
        worker.postMessage({ type: 'calculate-average' });
    });;
}
```

9. Create a `worker.js` file, assign the current context to a variable `global`, and declare variables named: `sharedIntArray`, `sharedInArraySlice`, `workerIndex`, `workerCount`, `startIndex`, and `endIndex`. Also, assign a function to the `onmessage` event:

```
// worker.js
const global = this;
let sharedIntArray;
let sharedIntArraylSlice;
let workerIndex;
let workerCount;
let startIndex;
let endIndex;

global.onmessage = (message) => {};
```

10. In the `onmessage` listener, get the data component of the `message` argument and switch on the `type` attribute:

```
global.onmessage = (message) => {
    const { data } = message;
    switch (data.type) {}
};
```

11. Add a case for `'load-array'` where we assign the array property of data to `sharedIntArray` after casting it as an `Int32Array`:

```
global.onmessage = (message) => {
    const { data } = message;
    switch (data.type) {
        case 'load-array':
            sharedIntArray = new Int32Array(data.array);
```

```
      break;
    }
  };
```

12. Add a case for `'load-indices'` that calculates the window of values that the current worker should work with, based on the current index and total number of workers:

```
global.onmessage = (message) => {
  const { data } = message;
  switch (data.type) {
    case 'load-array':
      sharedIntArray = new Int32Array(data.array);
      break;
    case 'load-indices':
      workerIndex = data.workerIndex;
      workerCount = data.workerCount;

      const windowSize = Math.floor(sharedIntArray.length /
      workerCount)
      startIndex = windowSize * workerIndex;
      const isLastWorker = workerIndex === workerCount - 1;
      endIndex = (isLastWorker) ? sharedIntArray.length :
      startIndex+windowSize;
      sharedIntArraySlice = sharedIntArray.slice(startIndex,
      endIndex);
      break;
  };
```

13. Add a case for `'calculate-sum'` that sums all the numbers in the array and posts the result back to the main thread:

```
global.onmessage = (message) => {
  const { data } = message;
  switch (data.type) {
  // ...

    case 'calculate-sum':
      const sum = sharedIntArraySlice.reduce((acc, number) =>
        acc + number
      , 0);
      sendResult('sum', sum);
      break;
  }
};
```

14. Add a case for `'calculate-average'` that averages all the numbers in the array and posts the result back to the main thread:

```
global.onmessage = (message) => {
  const { data } = message;
  switch (data.type) {
    //...
    case 'calculate-average':
      const total = sharedIntArraySlice.reduce((acc, number) =>
        acc + number
      , 0);
      const average = total / sharedIntArraySlice.length
      sendResult('average', average);
      break;
  }
};
```

15. Create a `sendResult` function that posts a `result`, a result type, and information about the current thread to the main thread:

```
function sendResult(type, result) {
  global.postMessage({
    type,
    result,
    workerIndex,
    startIndex,
    endIndex,
    windowSize: endIndex - startIndex - 1
  });
}
```

16. Start your Python web server and open the following link in your browser: `http://localhost:8000/`.

17. You should see the following output:

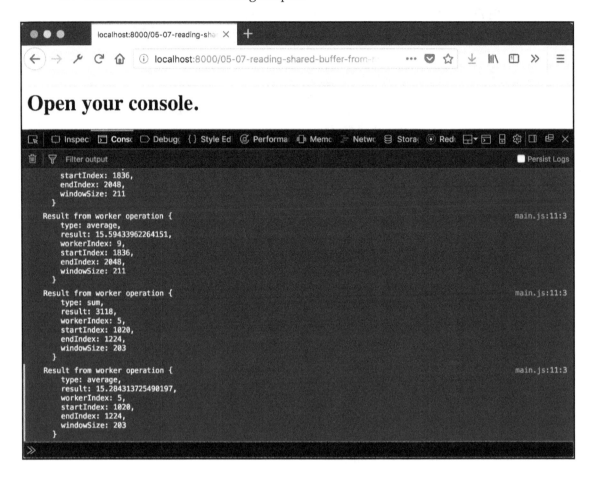

How it works...

Shared array buffers can be shared across any number of worker threads. In order to calculate portions of the result, we need to divide the results equitably between the threads. That's what the 'load-indices' case of the worker onMessage listener does.

We can use the size of the array and the total worker count to get the window size. We take the floor so that we don't go beyond the index of the array. This is also because you can't have a partial index: they are integers.

Next, we use the current worker index to get the `startIndex` (basically picking up where the previous worker left off). To get the end index, we need to know if this is the last worker. If not, we use the window size. If it is, we need to take all of the remaining values.

Once we have our array slice, each worker calculates the sums and averages of those portions as they would with the entire array. Then the results and the worker info are posted to the main thread.

Using Atomics to coordinate the use of shared memory

In the previous recipe, we used multiple workers to produce portions of a result. We could merge these results in the main thread. While valid, this approach doesn't take full advantage of parallel processing. It would be preferable if the workers could accumulate the results themselves.

Mutating shared memory in multiple parallel threads exposes the possibility of race conditions. This is when several operations need to occur in a specific order that is not enforced. Luckily, we can use the Atomics API to coordinate these operations.

In this recipe, we'll see how to use the Atomics API to accumulate results while avoiding race conditions.

Getting ready

This recipe assumes you already have a workspace that allows you to create and run ES modules in your browser. If you don't, please see the first two chapters.

How to do it...

1. Open your command-line application and navigate to your workspace.
2. Create a new folder named `05-08-use-atomics-to-coordinate`.
3. Copy or create an `index.html` that loads and runs a `main` function from `main.js`.

4. Create a `main.js` file. Create three shared array buffers: an input buffer and two output buffers (one `safe`, the other `unsafe`). The output buffers should be 32 bits in size:

```
// main.js
const NUMBER_COUNT = Math.pow(2, 10);
const BYTES_FOR_32_BIT = 4;
const ARRAY_SIZE = NUMBER_COUNT * BYTES_FOR_32_BIT;
const sab = new SharedArrayBuffer(ARRAY_SIZE);
const intBuffer = new Int32Array(sab);
const outSab = new SharedArrayBuffer(BYTES_FOR_32_BIT);
const unsafeSab = new SharedArrayBuffer(BYTES_FOR_32_BIT);
const workerCount = 256;
```

5. Declare a variable `workersFinishedCount` and set it to 0:

```
// main.js
let workersFinishedCount = 0;
```

6. Create a function named `onMessage`. This function increments `workersFinished`. If all the workers are finished, log the output of the two output arrays and log out a sum calculated locally:

```
//main.js
function onMessage(message) {
  workersFinishedCount++;
  if (workersFinishedCount === WORKER_COUNT) {
    const outIntBuffer = new Int32Array(outSab);
    const unsafeIntBuffer = new Int32Array(unsafeSab);
    console.log('Unsafe Sum: %s', unsafeIntBuffer[0]);
    console.log('Merged sum: %s', outIntBuffer[0]);
    const localSum = intBuffer.reduce((acc, curr) => acc +
curr,
      0);
    console.log('Local sum: %s', localSum);
  }
}
```

7. Create a main function that declares a `MAX_NUMBER`:

```
export function main() {
  const MAX_NUMBER = 32;
}
```

8. Next, create an array of workers of size `WORKER_COUNT`:

```
export function main() {
  // ...
  // create workers
</strong>  let workers = [];
  console.log('Creating workers.');
  for (let i = 0; i < WORKER_COUNT; i++) {
    const worker = new Worker('./worker.js');
    worker.onmessage = onMessage;
    workers = workers.concat(worker);
  }
}
```

9. Next, fill the input shared array buffer with random integers:

```
export function main() {
  // ...
  // fill with random numbers
  console.log('Filling Int buffer');
  intBuffer.forEach((value, index) => {
    intBuffer[index] = (Math.random() * MAX_NUMBER) + 1;
  });
}
```

10. Post these messages to each of the workers: `'load-shared-input'`, `'load-shared-output'`, `'load-indices'`, and `'calculate-sum'`:

```
export function main() {
  // ...
  workers.forEach((worker, workerIndex) => {
    worker.postMessage({ type: 'load-shared-input', input: sab
    });
    worker.postMessage({ type: 'load-shared-output', safe:
    outSab,
    unsafe: unsafeSab });
    worker.postMessage({ type: 'load-indices', workerIndex,
    workerCount: WORKER_COUNT });
    worker.postMessage({ type: 'calculate-sum' });
  });
}
```

11. Create a `worker.js` file, assign the current context to a `global` variable, declare variables named `sharedIntArray`, `resultArray`, `unsafeResultArray`, and `sharedInArraySlice`, and assign a function to the `onmessage` event:

```
// worker.js
const global = this;
let sharedIntArray;
let resultArray;
let unsafeResultArray;
let sharedIntArraylSlice;

global.onmessage = (message) => {};
```

12. In the `onmessage` listener, get the data component of the `message` argument and `switch` on the `type` attribute:

```
global.onmessage = (message) => {
  const { data } = message;
  switch (data.type) {}
};
```

13. Add a case for `'load-shared-input'`, where we assign the `input` property of data to `sharedIntArray` after casting it as an `Int32Array`:

```
global.onmessage = (message) => {
  const { data } = message;
  switch (data.type) {
    case 'load-shared-input':
      sharedIntArray = new Int32Array(data.input);
      break;
  }
};
```

14. Add a case for `'load-shared-output'`, where we assign the `safe` and `unsafe` properties of data to the corresponding result arrays after casting them as a `Int32Array`:

```
global.onmessage = (message) => {
  const { data } = message;
  switch (data.type) {
    case 'load-shared-output':
      resultArray = new Int32Array(data.safe);
      unsafeResultArray = new Int32Array(data.unsafe);
      break;
  }
};
```

15. Add a case for `'load-indices'` that calculates the window of values that the current worker should work with based on the current index and total number of workers:

```
global.onmessage = (message) => {
  const { data } = message;
  switch (data.type) {
    case 'load-array':
      sharedIntArray = new Int32Array(data.array);
      break;
    case 'load-indices':
      const { workerIndex, workerCount } = data;
      const windowSize = Math.floor(sharedIntArray.length /
      workerCount);
      const startIndex = windowSize * workerIndex;
      const lastWorker = workerIndex === workerCount - 1;
      const endIndex = (lastWorker) ? sharedIntArray.length :
      startIndex + windowSize;
      sharedIntArraySlice = sharedIntArray.slice(startIndex,
      endIndex);
      break;
  }
};
```

16. Add a case for `'calculate-sum'` that sums all the numbers in the array, updates `unsafeResultArray` directly, uses `Atomics.add` to update `resultArray`, and posts the result back to the main thread:

```
global.onmessage = (message) => {
  const { data } = message;
  switch (data.type) {
    // ...
    case 'calculate-sum':
      const sum = sharedIntArraySlice.reduce((acc, number) =>
        acc + number
      , 0);
      sendResult('sum', sum);
      break;
  }
};
```

17. Start your Python web server and open the following link in your browser: `http://localhost:8000/`.

18. You should see the following output:

How it works...

As we can see from the results, the value of `unsafeResultArray` has been corrupted by a race condition. It looks as if some of the values are missing. However, looking at the worker it appears as if we are adding the result as a single operation.

This isn't precisely true. The `+=` operator is actually three separate operations, a read, an addition, and a write operation. If you imagine that multiple workers reach this segment at the same time (we have 256 operating at once), then you can imagine how a race condition can occur.

Atomics prevent these errors from happening. `Atomic.add`, for example, operates as if +, = were a single operation. When a worker uses `Atomics.add` or any other method in the API, they can be sure that the values will not be written or read by another thread until the operation has been completed. That's why the safe sum always matches the sum calculated on the main thread, and the unsafe sum may be less.

 Because race conditions are non-deterministic, you may have to run this recipe several times in order to see a discrepancy between the safe and unsafe sums.

Using promises to provide a simple interface for a worker

So far, we've see how to use workers to perform a variety of tasks, but we've also seen that they can be cumbersome to use. This is unavoidable to some extent. However, we can provide nice interfaces to operations that are using workers with the tools we've already seen in in previous chapters.

In this recipe, we'll see how to use promises to create more familiar interfaces.

Getting ready

This recipe assumes you already have a workspace that allows you to create and run ES modules in your browser. If you don't, please see the first two chapters.

How to do it...

1. Open your command-line application, and navigate to your workspace.
2. Create a new folder named `05-09-using-promise-for-simple-interfaces`.
3. Copy or create an `index.html` that loads and runs a `main` function from `main.js`.
4. Create a `main.js` file, with an `async` function named `sumOnWorker`:

   ```
   // main.js
   async function sumOnWorker(array) {}
   ```

5. Inside `sumOnWorker`, return a new promise, wherein you create a new worker and bind the `onmessage` event listener, and post a message to the worker to calculate the sum:

   ```
   // main.jsfunction sumOnWorker(array) {
     return new Promise(function (resolve) {
       const worker = new Worker('./worker.js');
       worker.onmessage = (message) => {};
       worker.postMessage({ type: 'calculate-sum', array });
     });
   }
   ```

6. Inside the `onmessage` listener, log out the `type` and `result` properties of the message data, and resolve the `result`:

```
// main.js
async function sumOnWorker(array) {
  return new Promise(function (resolve) {
    const worker = new Worker('./worker.js');
    worker.onmessage = (message) => {
      const { type, result } = message.data;
      console.log('Completed operation (%s), result: %s',
        type,
        result
      );
      return resolve(result);
    };

    worker.postMessage({ type: 'calculate-sum', array });
  });
}
```

7. Create an `async` main function that creates three arrays of random numbers:

```
export function main() {
  const array0 = (new Array(10000)).fill().map(Math.random);
  const array1 = (new Array(1000)).fill().map(Math.random);
  const array2 = (new Array(100)).fill().map(Math.random);
}
```

8. Call `sumOnWorker` with each of the arrays, and log out the results:

```
export function main() {
  // ...
  sumOnWorker(array0).then((sum) => console.log('Array 0 sum:
%s', sum));
  sumOnWorker(array1).then((sum) => console.log('Array 1 sum:
%s', sum));
  sumOnWorker(array2).then((sum) => console.log('Array 2 sum:
%s', sum));;
}
```

9. Create a `worker.js` file, assign the current context to a variable `global`, and assign a function to the `onmessage` event:

```
// worker.js
const global = this;
global.onmessage = (message) => {};
```

10. In the `onmessage` listener, get the data component of the `message` argument and `switch` on the `type` attribute:

```
global.onmessage = (message) => {
  const { data } = message;
  switch (data.type) {}
};
```

11. Add a case for `'calculate-sum'`, where you calculate the sum of a posted array. Respond with the type or operation, and the resulting value:

```
global.onmessage = (message) => {
  const { data } = message;
  switch (data.type) {
    case 'calculate-sum':
      const sum = data.array.reduce((acc, number) => acc +
      number, 0);
      global.postMessage({ type: 'sum', result: sum });
      break;
  }
};
```

12. Start your Python web server and open the following link in your browser: `http://localhost:8000/`.

13. You should see the following output:

How it works...

We've seen in previous chapters how flexible composing promises and `async` functions can be. Doing so with workers is a natural extension. Consider an asynchronous AJAX request. This could be thought of as taking place in a worker. After all, it is being performed in a different thread of execution, but managed by the browser.

As long as success error conditions are handled properly, promises and `async` functions can be used to provide familiar interfaces to Web Workers. Having familiar and simple interfaces is crucial when integrating new technology with an existing code base.

6
Plain Objects

In this chapter, we will cover the following recipes:

- Using Object.assign to add properties to an object
- Using Object.entries to get iterable property-name pairs
- Using Object.is to compare two values
- Defining function properties as methods on a plain object
- Defining read-only props with Object.defineProperty
- Overriding read-only props with Object.defineProperty
- Creating a non-enumerable property with Object.defineProperty
- Creating an object using object structuring
- Picking values from an object using destructuring
- Using a spread operator to combine objects

Introduction

With all the new features made available in recent versions of ECMAScript, it's easy to lose sight of the fundamentals. The Object API, like others, has received plenty of updates. They may seem mundane compared to less familiar features (such as `SharedArrayBuffer`), but they allow you to create some interesting and useful behaviors.

In this chapter, we'll be looking at how to use the Object API to create rich relationships and interesting properties.

Using Object.assign to add properties to an object

Combining the properties from different objects is a fairly common task. Doing this value by value is limited and tedious, because each property has to be enumerated. This recipe demonstrates how to do the same thing with the `Object.assign` method.

Getting ready

This recipe assumes you already have a workspace that allows you to create and run ES modules in your browser. If you don't, please see the first two chapters.

How to do it...

1. Open your command-line application and navigate to your workspace.
2. Create a new folder named `06-01-object-assign-add-properties`.
3. Copy or create an `index.html` that loads and runs a `main` function from `main.js`.
4. Create a `main.js` file with a `main` function that creates two objects, and then uses `Object.assign` to combine them with another anonymous object:

```
// main.js
export function main() {
  const object = {};
  const otherObject = {
    foo: 'original value',
    bar: 'another value'
  }

  Object.assign(object, otherObject, {
    foo: 'override value'
  });

  console.log(object);
}
```

5. Start your Python web server and open the following link in your browser:
   `http://localhost:8000/`.
6. You will see the following output:

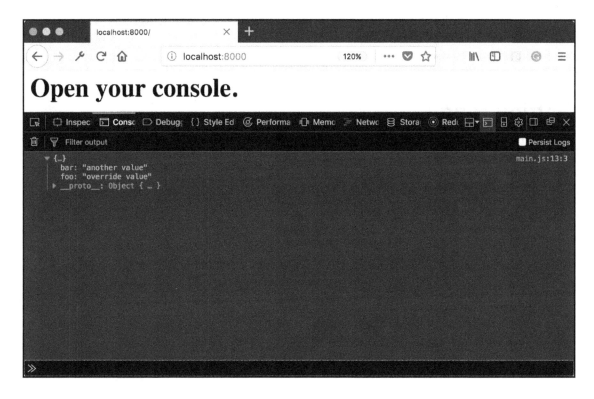

How it works...

The `Object` assign method iterates over all the properties of the objects passed to it. Then it assigns them to the leftmost object. Priority is given to properties on rightmost objects. So, you can see that the value of `foo` comes from the anonymous object. The leftmost object is mutated by the values from the right, while the other objects are left unchanged.

We'll see how to use the spread operator to accomplish the same task later on.

Using Object.entries to get iterable property-name pairs

`Object.assign` works well for copying properties from one object to another. However, we sometimes want to perform other operations based on the properties of an object. This recipe shows how to use `Object.entries` to get an iterable of an object's properties.

Getting ready

This recipe assumes you already have a workspace that allows you to create and run ES modules in your browser. If you don't, please see the first two chapters.

How to do it...

1. Open your command-line application and navigate to your workspace.
2. Create a new folder named `06-02-object-entries-to-get-iterable`.
3. Copy or create an `index.html` that loads and runs a `main` function from `main.js`.
4. Create a `main.js` with a function named `main` that creates an object then uses a `for-of` loop to loop over the result of `Object.entries`:

```
// main.js
export function main() {
  const object = {
    foo: Math.random(),
    bar: Math.random()
  };
  for (let [prop, value] of Object.entries(object)) {
    console.log(prop, value);
  }
}
```

5. Start your Python web server and open the following link in your browser: `http://localhost:8000/`.

6. You will see the following output:

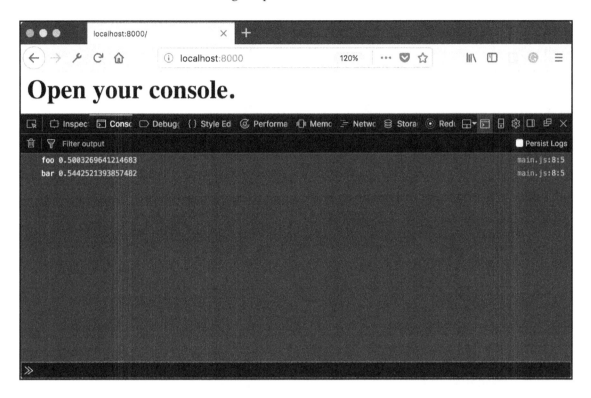

How it works...

`Object.entries` returns what is known as an iterable. These lists can be traversed with `for-of` loops. The items in this iterable are pairs of property names and values. The props are `foo` and `bar`, while the value entries are their corresponding values for those props.

The syntax `[prop, value]` destructures this pair into individual variables that are then logged out. Alternatively, we could reference the entry `prop` and `value` as the zero and 1 index of an array, but the destructured syntax is a little more direct. We'll look at destructuring in future recipes.

Using Object.is to compare two values

JavaScript has a complex relationship with equality. It is common knowledge that using === is preferable to == because it gives more predictable results, and in most cases === behaves as expected. Unfortunately, due to quirks in the JavaScript type system, there are some frustrating edge cases. In this recipe, we'll see how to use Object.is to get expected results for comparisons.

Getting ready

This recipe assumes you already have a workspace that allows you to create and run ES modules in your browser. If you don't, please see the first two chapters.

How to do it...

1. Open your command-line application and navigate to your workspace.
2. Create a new folder named 06-03-compare-with-object-is.
3. Copy or create an index.html that loads and runs a main function from main.js.
4. Create a main.js with a main function that makes a few illustrative comparisons:

```
// main.js
export function main() {
  const obj1 = {};
  const obj2 = {};

  console.log('obj1 === obj2', obj1 === obj2);
  console.log('obj1 is obj2', Object.is(obj1, obj2));
  console.log('obj2 === obj2', obj2 === obj2);
  console.log('obj2 is obj2', Object.is(obj2, obj2));
  console.log('undefined === undefined', undefined ===
  undefined);
  console.log('undefined is undefined', Object.is(undefined,
  undefined));
  console.log('null === undefined', null === undefined);
  console.log('null is undefined', Object.is(null, undefined));

  // Special cases (from MDN documentation)
  console.log('Special Cases:');
```

```
        console.log('0 === -0', 0 === -0);
        console.log('0 is -0', Object.is(0, -0));
        console.log('-0 === -0', -0 === -0);
        console.log('-0 is -0', Object.is(-0, -0));
        console.log('NaN === NaN', NaN === NaN);
        console.log('NaN is NaN', Object.is(NaN, NaN));
    }
```

5. Start your Python web server and open the following link in your browser: `http://localhost:8000/`.

6. You should see the following output displayed:

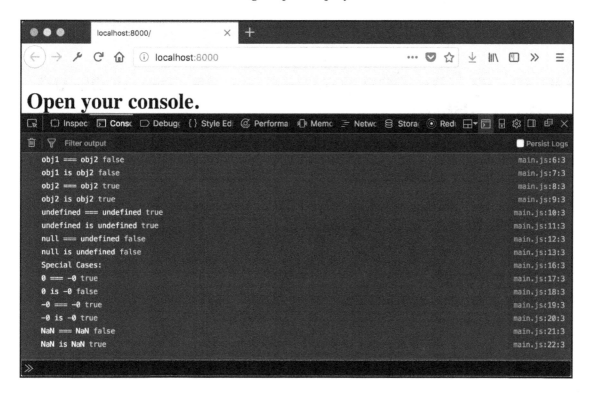

How it works...

The `Object.is` method has a different specification from the `===` operator. You can see that they agree most of the time, but there are certain edge cases where they disagree. The initial test cases (the `object`, `null`, and `undefined` comparison) all agree, but we start to see some differences when we hit corner cases. You can see the differences between a positive and negative zero comparison, as well as a NaN comparison.

 For more information, see the documentation on the Mozilla Developer page:
`https://developer.mozilla.org/en-US/docs/Web/JavaScript/`
`Reference/Global_Objects/Object/is`.

Defining function properties as methods on a plain object

Defining methods on object literals has always been possible with normal key-value pairs. More recent versions of ECMAScript have added a shorthand that mimics the syntax for defining methods on classes.

In this recipe, we'll see that we can create and override methods on object literals using either technique.

Getting ready

This recipe assumes you already have a workspace that allows you to create and run ES modules in your browser. If you don't, please see the first two chapters.

How to do it...

1. Open your command-line application and navigate to your workspace.
2. Create a new folder named `06-04-define-function-properties-as-method`.
3. Copy or create an `index.html` that loads and runs a `main` function from `main.js`.
4. Create a `main.js` with a function named `main` that defines two methods with the property and method syntax, overrides them, and calls them before and after override:

```
// main.js
export function main() {
    const obj = {
      method0: function() {
        console.log('Hello, from method one.')
      },
        method1() {
        console.log('Hello, from method one.')
      }
    };
    obj.method0();
    obj.method1();

    obj.method0 = () => console.log('Override of method 0.');
    obj.method1 = () => console.log('Override of method 1.');
    obj.method0();
    obj.method1();
}
```

5. Start your Python web server and open the following link in your browser: `http://localhost:8000/`.

6. You should see the following output displayed:

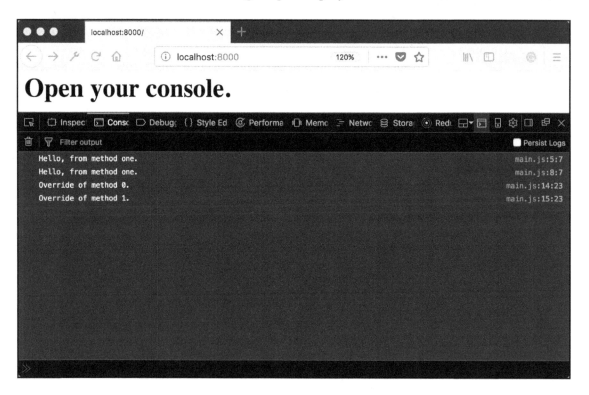

How it works...

As we saw previously, the two syntaxes are equivalent. The two methods are defined as properties with function values, and because they don't have any attributes that prevent it, they can be overridden. Both `method0` and `method1` are defined on the initial object and executed immediately thereafter.

Next, we assign a new function value to those properties of the same object. So when they are called again, the new functions are executed, rather than the originals.

In future recipes, we'll see how to prevent this kind of overriding.

Defining read-only props with Object.defineProperty

It's not always ideal to have methods that can be overridden. By default, properties that are assigned to an object can be reassigned. We need another option to add functions to an object so they won't be changed.

In this recipe, we'll see how to add non-writable properties to an object with `Object.defineProperty`.

Getting ready

This recipe assumes you already have a workspace that allows you to create and run ES modules in your browser. If you don't, please see the first two chapters.

How to do it...

1. Open your command-line application and navigate to your workspace.
2. Create a new folder named `06-05-define-readonly-props`.
3. Copy or create an `index.html` that loads and runs a `main` function from `main.js`.
4. Create a `main.js` file with a `main` function that defines a non-writable property, and then tries to write to it:

```
export function main() {
 const obj = {};

 Object.defineProperty(obj, 'method1',{
   writable: false,
   value: () => {
     console.log('Hello, from method one.')
   }
 });
 obj.method1();

 // throws error
 obj.method1 = () => console.log('Override of method 1.');
}
```

5. Start your Python web server and open the following link in your browser: `http://localhost:8000/`.

6. You should see the following output displayed:

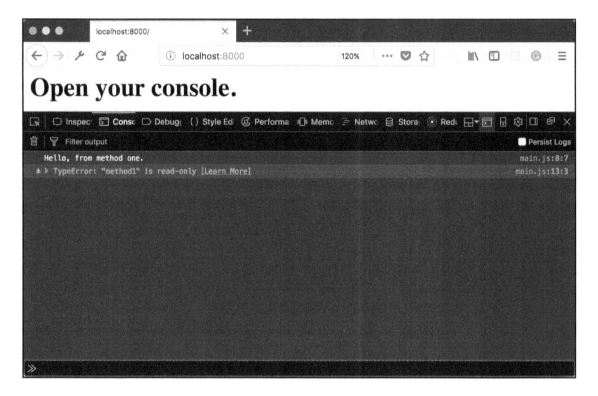

How it works...

In this recipe, we see that object properties are not simple key-value pairs. They have attributes that governern their behavior. One of these properties is writable. This property means that we can reassign the value afterwards. By default, this property is set to true; using `Object.defineProperty` we can see other values.

We'll see how other properties can be used to control other behaviors.

Overriding read-only props with Object.defineProperty

Creating a non-writable property isn't the final word. In some cases, it is still possible to rewrite these properties. Thankfully, it is not something that is likely to be done by accident. In this recipe, we'll see how to define and redefine non-writable props with `Object.define`.

Getting ready

This recipe assumes you already have a workspace that allows you to create and run ES modules in your browser. If you don't, please see the first two chapters.

How to do it...

1. Open your command-line application and navigate to your workspace.
2. Create a new folder named `06-06-redefine-read-only-props`.
3. Copy or create an `index.html` that loads and runs a `main` function from `main.js`.
4. Create a `main.js` file with a `main` function that creates an object. Define a configurable, non-writable property named `prop1` with a random value:

```
export function main() {
  const obj = {};

  Object.defineProperty(obj, 'prop1',{
    writable: false,
    configurable: true,
    value: Math.random()
  });
  console.log(obj.prop1)
}
```

5. Redefine that property as another `random` value and change configurable to `false`:

```
export function main() {
  // ...
  Object.defineProperty(obj, 'prop1',{
```

```
        writable: false,
        configurable: false,
        value: Math.random()
    });
    console.log(obj.prop1)}
```

6. Attempt to redefine the property a third time:

```
export function main() {
    // ...
    // throws error
    Object.defineProperty(obj, 'prop1',{
        value: Math.random()
    });
}
```

7. Start your Python web server and open the following link in your browser: http://localhost:8000/.

8. You should see the following output displayed:

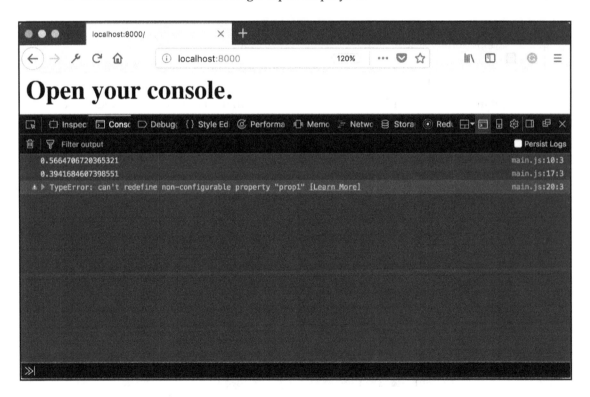

How it works...

Writable is only part of the equation. Setting writable to false means that the property can be reassigned normally. By default, it cannot be redefined with `Object.defineProperty`. However, if `configurable` is set to true, then the property can be redefined. Once the `configurable` attribute is set to false, then we can no longer redefine it.

Creating a non-enumerable property with Object.defineProperty

We've seen in previous recipes how to avoid having properties overridden. There are situations where we might not want a property to be read. Recall the `Object.entries` method, which creates an iterator of all the properties and values on the object. Well, that's not precisely true. It creates an iterator of all the `enumerable` properties.

In this recipe, we'll see how to create properties that won't be included in the iterator.

Getting ready

This recipe assumes you already have a workspace that allows you to create and run ES modules in your browser. If you don't, please see the first two chapters.

How to do it...

1. Open your command-line application and navigate to your workspace.
2. Create a new folder named `06-07-non-enumerable-props`.
3. Copy or create an `index.html` that loads and runs a `main` function from `main.js`.

4. Create a `main.js` file with a `main` function that creates an object with key-value pairs of books and authors:

```
// main.js
export function main() {
  const bookAuthors = {
    "Star's End": "Cassandra Rose Clarke",
    "Three Body Problem": "Liu Cixin",
    "Houston Houston, Do You Read?": "James Tiptree Jr."
  };
}
```

5. Define two properties, one an `enumerable` with a random value and another non-enumerable with a function as the value:

```
export function main() {
  // ...
  Object.defineProperty(bookAuthors, 'visibleProp', {
    enumerable: true,
    value: Math.random()
  });

  Object.defineProperty(bookAuthors, 'invisibleProp', {
    value: () => console.log('This function is hidden.')
  });

  for (const [prop, value] of Object.entries(bookAuthors)) {
    console.log(prop, value)
  }
  bookAuthors.invisibleProp();
}
```

6. Start your Python web server and open the following link in your browser: `http://localhost:8000/`.

7. You should see the following output displayed:

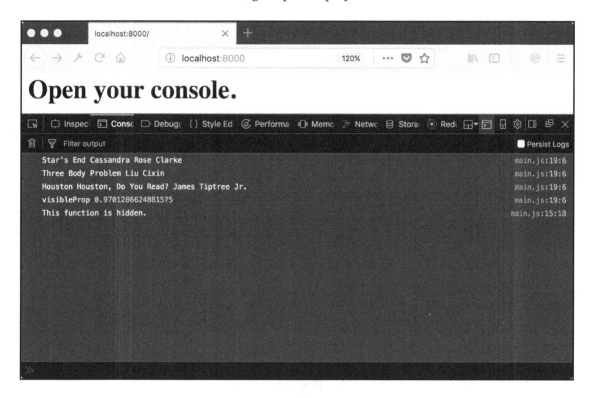

How it works...

The key values defined as literals on the object are enumerable as before. The next two properties are more interesting. The first property, visibleProp, explicitly sets the enumerable attribute to true, and appears in the list. The invisibleProp property is not explicitly set; the default value is false. Only the enumerable properties appear in the iterator.

Creating an object using object structuring

Pulling attributes from an object is yet another repetitive task. There seems to be unnecessary repetition. Newer versions of ECMAScript include a syntactic feature that makes this process less onerous. This recipe demonstrates how to use object destructuring to pull new variables from object props.

Getting ready

This recipe assumes you already have a workspace that allows you to create and run ES modules in your browser. If you don't, please see the first two chapters.

How to do it...

1. Open your command-line application and navigate to your workspace.
2. Create a new folder named `06-08-pick-values-from-object-destructuring`.
3. Copy or create an `index.html` that loads and runs a `main` function from `main.js`.
4. Create a `main.js` file. Create a main function that creates a new object then creates new constants from the properties therein:

```
// main.js
export function main() {
  const object = {
    prop1: 'some value',
    prop2: 'some other value',
    objectProp: { foo: 'bar' }
  };

  const { prop1, prop2, objectProp } = object;
  console.log(prop1);
  console.log(prop2);
  console.log(objectProp);
}
```

5. Start your Python web server and open the following link in your browser: `http://localhost:8000/`.

6. You should see the following output displayed:

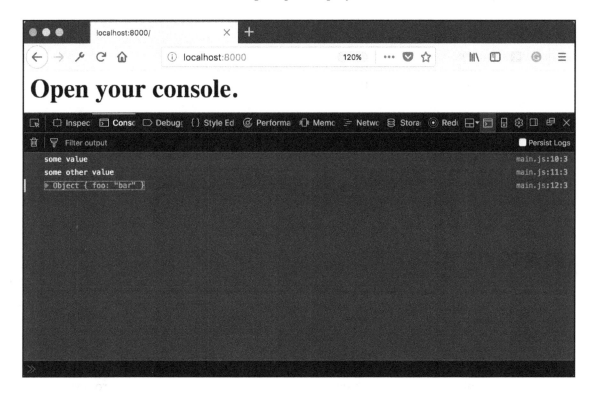

How it works...

Destructuring is syntactic shorthand. The names of the variables are used to reference properties on the object. The values are assigned to the variable of the corresponding name.

Picking values from an object using destructuring

Bundling multiple properties into a single object is another common task in JavaScript that can be really tedious. More recent versions of ECMAScript have added a new bit of syntax to make this more convenient.

In this recipe, we'll see how to use this new syntax to create an object from existing variables.

Getting ready

This recipe assumes you already have a workspace that allows you to create and run ES modules in your browser. If you don't, please see the first two chapters.

How to do it...

1. Open your command-line application and navigate to your workspace.
2. Create a new folder named `06-09-create-objects-with-structuring`.
3. Copy or create an `index.html` that loads and runs a `main` function from `main.js`.
4. Create a `main.js` file with an `async` function named `main`, which creates several constants and then uses object structuring to create an object with properties of the corresponding names and values:

```
// main.js
export function main() {
  const prop1 = 'some value';
  const prop2 = 'some other value';
  const objectProp = { foo: 'bar' };
  const object = { prop1, prop2, objectProp };

  console.log(object);
}
```

5. Start your Python web server and open the following link in your browser: `http://localhost:8000/`.

6. You should see the following output displayed:

How it works...

Like the previous recipe, the syntax uses the names of the variables between the curly braces to determine the property name on the object. Each of the properties is created with the variable name and value of the corresponding constant.

Using a spread operator to combine objects

In a previous recipe, we saw how to use `Object.assign` to combine objects. It gets the job done, but by using newer ECMAScript syntax we can do this in a more compact way. In this recipe, we'll see how to use the new spread operator to combine objects.

Getting ready

This recipe assumes you already have a workspace that allows you to create and run ES modules in your browser. If you don't, please see the first two chapters.

How to do it...

1. Open your command-line application and navigate to your workspace.
2. Create a new folder named `06-10-spread-operator-combine`.
3. Copy or create an `index.html` that loads and runs a `main` function from `main.js`.
4. Create a `main.js` file with an `async` function named `main`, which creates a couple of objects and a constant. It then uses the spread operator and object structuring to combine them into a single object:

```
// main.js
export function main() {
  const object1 = {
    prop1: 'some value',
    prop2: 'some other value',
  }
  const object2 = {
    prop2: 'some overriding value',
    objectProp: { foo: 'bar' }
  }
  const anotherProp = Math.random();

  const combinedObject = { ...object1, ...object2, anotherProp
};
  console.log(combinedObject);
}
```

5. Start your Python web server and open the following link in your browser: `http://localhost:8000/`.

6. You should see the following output displayed:

How it works...

The spread operator spreads out the `enumerable` properties of an object so that they are all referenced when structuring the new object. Like `Object.assign`, the values are given priority from right to left, and the last property is handled in the sane way as with object structuring in a prior recipe.

Creating Classes

7

In this chapter, we will cover the following recipes:

- Creating a new class
- Assigning properties with constructor arguments
- Defining methods on a class
- Checking the instance type with instanceOf
- Using getters to create read-only properties
- Using setters to encapsulate values
- Using static methods to work with all instances

Introduction

Creating and extending similar objects has always been possible with JavaScript's prototypical inheritance model. By using the `new` operator and adding prototype properties, we can create structures that behave like classes.

ECMAScript 2015 introduced class syntax as a friendlier way to work with prototypical inheritance. It has been argued that this *syntactic sugar* is not worth the overhead of having two ways to implement OOP structures. However, I would argue that class provides a more concise way of expressing the same idea, and is a net benefit. As we'll see in this chapter and the next, the class syntax makes it easier to express sophisticated OOP relationships.

Creating a new class

The most fundamental task class can be used for is, of course, creating a new class. This recipe shows the simple syntax for defining and instantiating a new class.

Getting ready

This recipe assumes you already have a workspace that allows you to create and run ES modules in your browser. If you don't, please see the first two chapters.

How to do it...

1. Open your command-line application and navigate to your workspace.
2. Create a new folder named `07-01-create-a-new-class`.
3. Copy or create an `index.html` that loads and runs a `main` function from `main.js`.
4. Create a `main.js` file that defines a new class named `Rocket` and a `main` function that creations two instances and logs them out:

```
// main.js
class Rocket {}

export function main() {
  const saturnV = new Rocket();
  const falconHeavy = new Rocket();
  console.log(saturnV);
  console.log(falconHeavy);
}
```

5. Start your Python web server and open the following link in your browser: `http://localhost:8000/`.
6. You will see the following output:

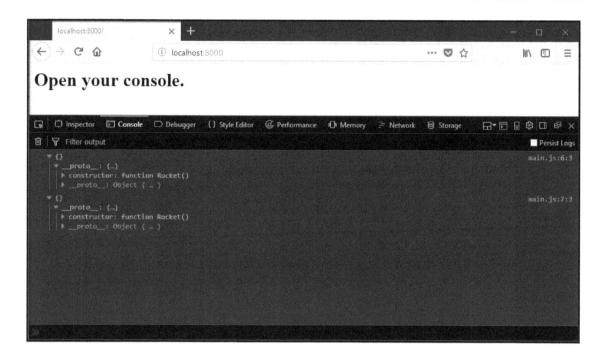

How it works...

The `classRocket {}` syntax is the equivalent to creating a function named `Rocket` (notice the `constructor` value of the logged object). This means that, in JavaScript, instances of `Rocket` can be created with the `new` operator. This creates an object based on the prototype.

We'll see how to make some more interesting objects in future recipes.

Assigning properties with constructor arguments

Now that we have a new class, it's time to start differentiating instances. In this recipe, we'll see how to assign properties when instances are created, via constructor arguments.

Getting ready

This recipe assumes you already have a workspace that allows you to create and run ES modules in your browser. If you don't, please see the first two chapters.

How to do it...

1. Open your command-line application and navigate to your workspace.
2. Create a new folder named `07-02-assigning-constructor-props`.
3. Copy or create an `index.html` that loads and runs a `main` function from `main.js`.
4. Create a `main.js` file that creates a new class named `Rocket`. Add a `constructor` method that takes a single argument, `name`, and assigns it to a property of the same name in the body of the method:

```
// main.js
class Rocket {
  constructor(name) {
    this.name = name;
  }
}
```

5. Create a `main` function that creates two instances and logs them out with their property:

```
// main.js
export function main() {
  const saturnV = new Rocket('Saturn V');
  const falconHeavy = new Rocket('Falcon Heavy');
  console.log(saturnV.name, saturnV);
  console.log(falconHeavy.name, falconHeavy);
}
```

6. Start your Python web server and open the following link in your browser: `http://localhost:8000/`.

7. You should see the following output displayed:

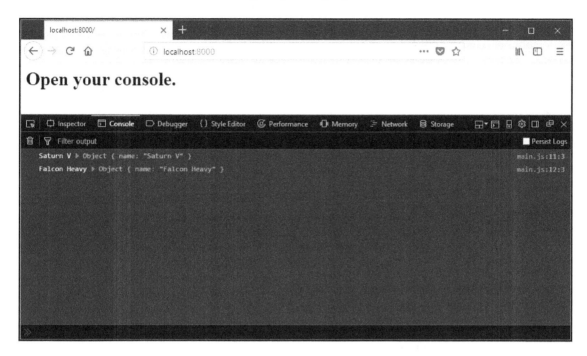

How it works...

As we saw in the previous recipe, the class syntax creates an empty `constructor` function if none is defined. A `constructor` is a method that is called immediately after a class is instantiated. Here, we create a new `Rocket` instance as follows:

```
const saturnV = new Rocket('Saturn V');
```

This means that the name property is actually assigned before that rocket instance is returned from the `new` expression and assigned to `saturnV`.

In this recipe, we define the `constructor`. The context of the `constructor` function, the value of `this`, is the instance of the new object. Therefore, when we assign the `name` property of `this`, it is set on that new instance.

Defining methods on a class

Classes that hold values are not particularly interesting. We also want them to be able to have some behaviors that act as interfaces to the outside world. In this recipe, we'll see how to add methods to a class.

Getting ready

This recipe assumes you already have a workspace that allows you to create and run ES modules in your browser. If you don't, please see the first two chapters.

How to do it...

1. Open your command-line application and navigate to your workspace.
2. Create a new folder named `07-03-defining-methods`.
3. Copy or create an `index.html` that loads and runs a `main` function from `main.js`.
4. Create a `main.js` with a class named `Rocket`, which assigns a `name` property upon construction:

```
// main.js
class Rocket {
  constructor(name) {
    this.name = name;
  }
}
```

5. Add a method named `takeoff` that accepts an option countdown argument. The body of the method should log a message before and after a timeout:

```
// main.js
class Rocket {
  // ...
  takeOff(countdown = 1000) {
    console.log(this.name + ' starting countdown.');
    setTimeout(() => {
      console.log(`Blastoff! ${this.name} has taken off`);
    }, countdown);
  }
}
```

6. Add a `main` function that creates two instances and then calls their `takeOff` methods:

```
// main.js
export function main() {
  const saturnV = new Rocket('Saturn V');
  const falconHeavy = new Rocket('Falcon Heavy');
  saturnV.takeOff(500);
  falconHeavy.takeOff();
}
```

7. Start your Python web server and open the following link in your browser: `http://localhost:8000/`.

8. You will see the following output:

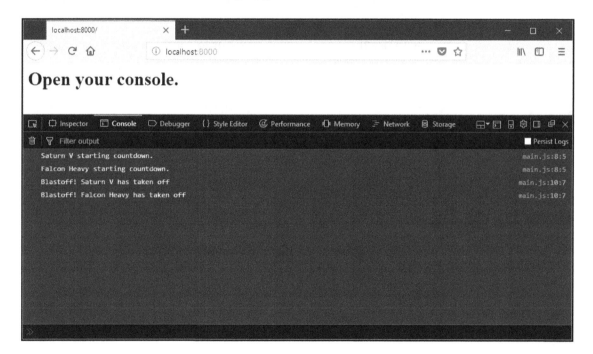

How it works...

Adding methods to the body of a class definition is the same as attaching properties to the prototype of a function, with functions as their values. This means that those properties are added as properties to the instance of the new object. When these methods are called, the context (the value of `this`) is the current instance.

Checking instance type with instanceOf

There are many situations, such as argument validation, where we'll want to check the class of an object. Because JavaScript is not statically typed, we can't guarantee that a function receives an argument of the correct type before the program starts, and we need to check at runtime.

In this recipe, we'll see how to use the `instanceOf` operator to check an object's prototype at runtime.

Getting ready

This recipe assumes you already have a workspace that allows you to create and run ES modules in your browser. If you don't, please see the first two chapters.

How to do it...

1. Open your command-line application and navigate to your workspace.
2. Create a new folder named `07-04-checking-with-instanceof`.
3. Copy or create an `index.html` that loads and runs a `main` function from `main.js`.

4. Create a `main.js` with two identical classes, `Rocket` and `InactiveRocket`:

```
// main.js class Rocket {
  constructor(name) {
    this.name = name;
  }
}

class InactiveRocket {
  constructor(name) {
    this.name = name;
  }
}
```

5. Create a function named `printRocketType` that uses `instanceOf` to distinguish between rocket classes:

```
// main.js class Rocket {
function printRocketType(rocket) {
  if (rocket instanceof InactiveRocket) {
    console.log(rocket.name + ' is an inactive rocket');
  } else {
    console.log(rocket.name + ' is active');
  }
}
```

6. Create a `main` function that creates rockets of either class and then calls `printRocketType` on both of them:

```
// main.js
export function main() {
  const saturnV = new InactiveRocket('Saturn V');
  const falconHeavy = new Rocket('Falcon Heavy');

  [saturnV, falconHeavy].forEach(printRocketType);
}
```

7. Start your Python web server and open the following link in your browser: `http://localhost:8000/`.

8. You should see the following output displayed:

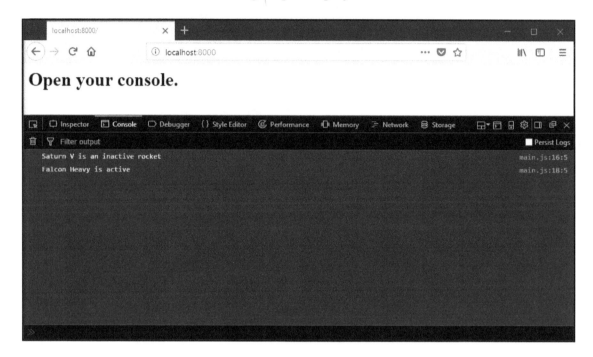

How it works...

The `instanceOf` operator compares a prototype of the left-hand value with the right-hand value. If the two match, the expression is evaluated as true, otherwise it evaluates as false. Thus, we can use it in a conditional expression.

Using getters to create read-only properties

We don't always want a property to be writable. In previous recipes, we saw how to create a read-only property on an object. In this recipe, we'll see how to use the `get` keyword to do this in the context of a class body.

Getting ready

This recipe assumes you already have a workspace that allows you to create and run ES modules in your browser. If you don't, please see the first two chapters.

How to do it...

1. Open your command-line application and navigate to your workspace.
2. Create a new folder named `07-05-getters-read-only`.
3. Copy or create an `index.html` that loads and runs a `main` function from `main.js`.
4. Create a `main.js` file with the `Rocket` class that defines a read only property:

```
class Rocket {
  constructor(name) {
    this.name = name;
  }

  get readOnlyValue() {
    return 'Cant' touch this.';
  }
}
```

5. Create a `main` function that creates an instance of the `Rocket` class. Read from the writable and read-only properties, then try to write to them:

```
export function main() {
  const saturnV = new Rocket('Saturn V');

  console.log(saturnV.name);
  saturnV.name = 'Saturn Five';
  console.log(saturnV.name);

  console.log(saturnV.readOnlyValue);
  // throws error
  saturnV.readOnlyValue = 'somethingElse';
}
```

6. Start your Python web server and open the following link in your browser: `http://localhost:8000/`.

7. You should see the following output displayed:

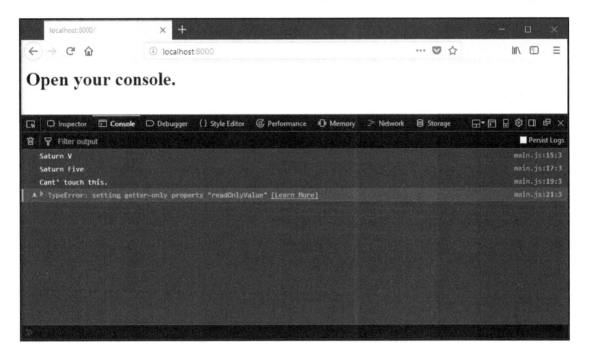

How it works...

Using the `get` keyword creates a read-only property that has a function for a value. We return a string from that function, so that, when the property is read, that value is returned. However, because it is read-only, a run-time error is thrown when we try to write to it.

Using setters to encapsulate values

In the previous recipe, we saw how to prevent values from being written. Sometimes however, we don't want to prevent a property from being written to. Rather, we want to control how it is written to. In this recipe, we'll see how to use `set` to control the writing of a property.

Getting ready

This recipe assumes you already have a workspace that allows you to create and run ES modules in your browser. If you don't, please see the first two chapters.

How to do it...

1. Open your command-line application and navigate to your workspace.
2. Create a new folder named `07-06-setters-encapsulate`.
3. Copy or create an `index.html` that loads and runs a `main` function from `main.js`.
4. Create a `main.js` file with a `Rocket` class that writes a `_secretName` property upon construction:

```
class Rocket {
  constructor(name) {
    this._secretName = name;
  }
}
```

5. Add a getter and setter for a `name` property and only update it if the `newValue` is a string:

```
class Rocket {
  // ...
  get name() {
    return this._secretName;
  }

  set name(newValue) {
    if (typeof newValue === 'string') {
      this._secretName = newValue;
    } else {
      console.error('Invalid name: ' + newValue)
    }
  }
}
```

6. Create a `main` function that tries to set the `name` property to different values:

```
export function main() {
  const saturnV = new Rocket('Saturn V');
  console.log(saturnV.name)
  saturnV.name = 'Saturn Five';
  console.log(saturnV.name)
  saturnV.name = 5;
  console.log(saturnV.name)
}
```

7. Start your Python web server and open the following link in your browser: `http://localhost:8000/`.

8. You should see the following output displayed:

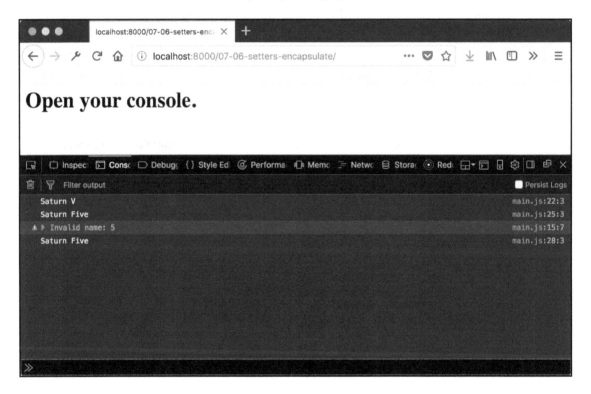

How it works...

Like the `get` keyword, the `set` keyword calls a function property when a property is written to. Instead of setting the value directly, we are able to perform a type check. If the `newValue` is a string, it is written as normal. Otherwise, we log an error, and do not set the value of the secret property.

Obviously, `_secretName` can be written directly. This has to be solved through documentation. Users of a library should only be using the public interface. They deviate at their own risk!

Using static methods to work with all instances

It can be a good idea to organize methods on a class, rather than on an instance of a class. One example is the **Manager** pattern. This pattern is useful when an object is expensive to create, or will be reused a lot.

In this recipe, we'll see how to use the `static` keyword to create a map for reusing instances of the `Rocket` class.

Getting ready

This recipe assumes you already have a workspace that allows you to create and run ES modules in your browser. If you don't, please see the first two chapters.

How to do it...

1. Open your command-line application and navigate to your workspace.
2. Create a new folder named `07-07-static-methods-on-all-instances`.
3. Copy or create an `index.html` that loads and runs a `main` function from `main.js`.

4. Create a `main.js` file with an empty object `rocketMap` and a class `Rocket`:

```
//main.js
let rocketMap = {};

class Rocket {}
```

5. Create a static method named `find` that looks up rockets by string on the `Rocket` class:

```
class Rocket {
  // ...
  static find (name) {
    return rocketMap[name];
  }
}
```

6. Add a construction that assigns a name property, and assigns the instance to the `rocketMap`:

```
class Rocket {
  // ...
  constructor (name) {
    this.name = name;
    rocketMap[name] = this;
  }
}
```

7. Create a `main` function that compares created instances of `Rocket` with results of the static `find` method:

```
//main.js
export function main() {
  const saturnV = new Rocket('Saturn V');
  const falconHeavy = new Rocket('Falcon Heavy');

  console.log('Is Saturn V?', saturnV === Rocket.find('Saturn
  V'));
  console.log('Is Falcon Heavy?', falconHeavy ===
  Rocket.find('Saturn V'));
  console.log('Is Same Rocket?', Rocket.find('Saturn V') ===
  Rocket.find('Saturn V'));
}
```

8. Start your Python web server and open the following link in your browser: `http://localhost:8000/`.

9. You should see the following output displayed:

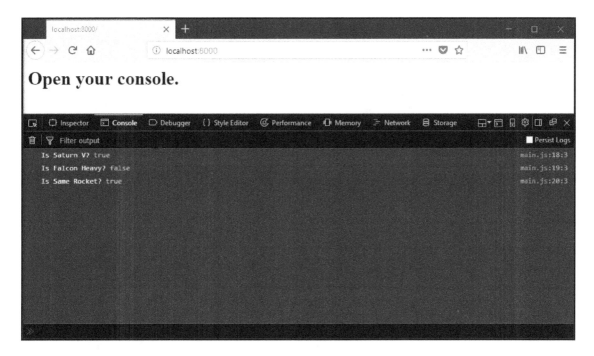

How it works...

The static keyword means that the function will be a property of the `Rocket` class, rather than an instance. This is the same as setting a function property directly on a function, rather than on its prototype. Thus, we call the function as a property of the class, not an instance.

Inheritance and Composition 8

In this chapter, we will cover the following recipes:

- Extending a class
- Assigning additional properties with constructor arguments
- Overriding parent class instance methods
- Overriding parent class static methods
- Calling super methods
- Using composition rather than inheritance to add behavior
- Using mix-ins to add behavior
- Passing a class as an argument
- Checking class inheritance with Object.getPrototypeOf
- Using throw to simulate abstract classes

Introduction

In the previous chapter, we saw how to use the new class syntax to implement behavior that was only slightly more difficult to implement directly with a prototype. A developer could be excused for thinking that this complexity of the language was not worth it. After all, it's only a line (or perhaps a character) or two extra to get the same behavior.

The real advantage of using the new ES6 class syntax to create object prototypes is revealed when more complicated structures and techniques are used. In essence, we'll see that it's much easier to understand code when the behavior is defined with keywords, rather than context-sensitive operators.

In this chapter, we'll look at how to implement some more sophisticated behaviors using classes.

Extending a class

Extending classes can be used to allow for new behaviors, while adhering to common interfaces. While it's not always the best way to organize relationships between objects, there are many situations where extension (sometimes called inheritance) is the most effective way to structure behavior.

In this recipe, we'll see a very simple example of extension.

Getting ready

This recipe assumes you already have a workspace that allows you to create and run ES modules in your browser. If you don't, please see the first two chapters.

How to do it...

1. Open your command-line application and navigate to your workspace.
2. Create a new folder named 08-01-extending-classes.
3. Copy or create an index.html that loads and runs a main function from main.js.
4. Create a main.js file that defines a new class named Rocket that takes a constructor argument name and assigns it to an instance property:

```
// main.js
class Rocket {
  constructor(name) {
    this.name = name;
  }
}
```

5. Create a class named InactiveRocket that extends the Rocket class:

```
// main.js
class InactiveRocket extends Rocket {}
```

6. Create a `main` function that creates instances of both classes and logs out their names:

```
// main.js
export function main() {
  const saturnV = new InactiveRocket('Saturn V');
  const falconHeavy = new Rocket('Falcon Heavy');

  console.log(saturnV.name, ' is a rocket.');
  console.log(falconHeavy.name, ' is also a rocket.');
}
```

7. Start your Python web server and open the following link in your browser: `http://localhost:8000/`.

8. You will see output like the following:

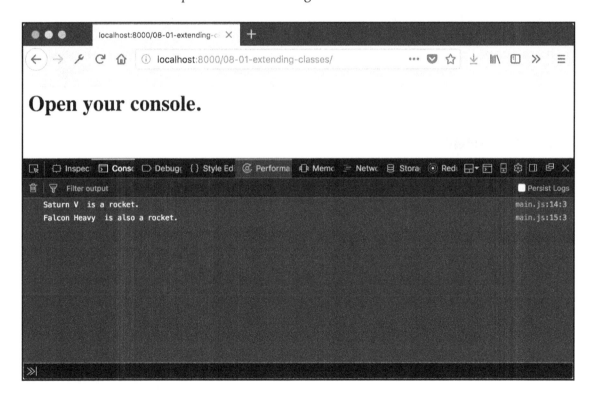

How it works...

The class InactiveRocket extends Rocket. This means that all of the properties on the prototype of Rocket end up on the instance of InactiveRocket unless they are overridden. The constructor is special, but it is also a property on the Rocket prototype. Therefore, when the two instances are created, the Rocket class constructor is executed for both the Rocket and InactiveRocket instances. So, we see the name property assigned on both instances.

We'll see how to override methods and other behaviors in future recipes.

Assigning additional properties with constructor arguments

If we are extending a class, we'll want it to be a little bit different. Otherwise, what's the point of extending it? In this recipe we'll differentiate a child class by adding additional properties.

Getting ready

This recipe assumes you already have a workspace that allows you to create and run ES modules in your browser. If you don't, please see the first two chapters.

How to do it...

1. Open your command line application and navigate to your workspace.
2. Create a new folder named 08-02-additional-constructor-args.

3. Create a `main.js` file that defines a new class named `Rocket` that takes a constructor argument `name` and assigns it to an instance property:

```
// main.js
class Rocket {
  constructor(name) {
    this.name = name;
  }
}
```

4. Create a class named `InactiveRocket` that extends the `Rocket` class, and assigns an additional `lastFlown` property in the constructor:

```
// main.js
class InactiveRocket extends Rocket {
  constructor(name, lastFlown) {
    super(name);
    this.lastFlown = lastFlown;
  }
}
```

5. Create a `main` function that creates instances of both classes and logs out their names, and the `lastFlown` property of the `InactiveRocket`:

```
// main.js
export function main() {
  const saturnV = new InactiveRocket('Saturn V', new Date('May
  14,1973'));
  const falconHeavy = new Rocket('Falcon Heavy');
  console.log(falconHeavy.name + ' is a Rocket');
  console.log(saturnV.name + ' is an inactive rocket');
  console.log(`${saturnV.name} was last flown:
  ${rocket.lastFlown}`);
}
```

6. Start your Python web server and open the following link in your browser: `http://localhost:8000/`.

7. You should see output like the following:

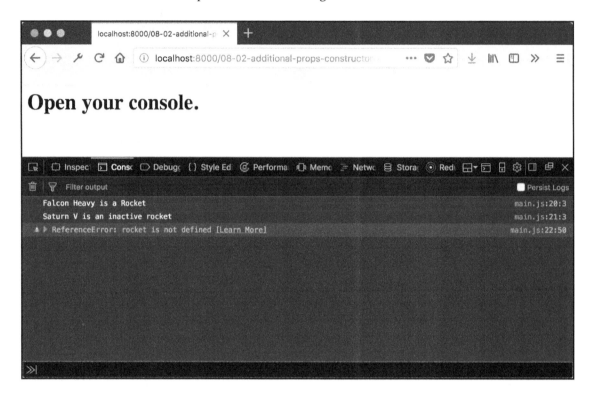

How it works...

This recipe differs from the previous simple extension example. By implementing a constructor on `InactiveRocket`, we are able to pass a different set of arguments. The `lastFlown` property is unique to `InactiveRocket`. Thus, we see that property on instances of `InactiveRocket`, but not on instances of `Rocket`.

You'll notice that the `super` method is called in the constructor of `InactiveRocket`. This manually executes the `Rocket` constructor for the current instance. That is why the `name` property is also attached. If we did not execute `super`, then the `Rocket` constructor would not have been called.

In this way, we've kept the properties from the parent class `Rocket` as well as adding an additional property to the `InactiveRocket` child class.

Overriding parent class instance methods

Ideally, classes contain more than just properties. Well-designed classes also define behavior. Thus, sub-classes should also be extending behavior, not just adding additional properties.

In this recipe, we'll see how to override methods from a parent class.

Getting ready

This recipe assumes you already have a workspace that allows you to create and run ES modules in your browser. If you don't, please see the first two chapters.

How to do it...

1. Open your command line application and navigate to your workspace.
2. Create a new folder named `08-03-defining-methods`.
3. Copy or create an `index.html` that loads and runs a `main` function from `main.js`.
4. Create a `main.js` file that defines a new class named `Rocket`. Add a constructor that takes a constructor argument `name` and assigns it to an instance property. Then, define a simple `print` method:

```js
// main.js
class Rocket {
  constructor(name) {
    this.name = name;
  }

  print() {
    console.log(this.name + ' is a Rocket');
  }
}
```

5. Create a class named `InactiveRocket` that extends the `Rocket` class and assigns an additional `lastFlow` property in the constructor. Then, override the `print` method to include the new property:

```javascript
// main.js
class InactiveRocket extends Rocket {
  constructor(name, lastFlown) {
    super(name);
    this.lastFlown = lastFlown;
  }

  print() {
    console.log(this.name + ' is an inactive rocket');
    console.log(`${this.name} was last flown:
    ${this.lastFlown}`);
  }
}
```

6. Create a `main` function that creates instances of both classes and calls the `print` method of both:

```javascript
// main.js
export function main() {
  const saturnV = new InactiveRocket('Saturn V', new Date('May
  14,1973'));
  const falconHeavy = new Rocket('Falcon Heavy');

  [saturnV, falconHeavy].forEach((r) => r.print());
}
```

7. Start you Python web server and open the following link in your browser: `http://localhost:8000/`.

8. You should see output like the following:

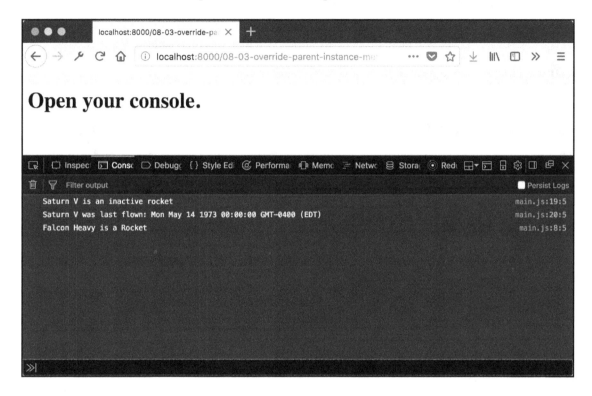

How it works...

Adding methods to the body of a class definition is the same as attaching properties to the prototype of a function, with functions as their values. This means that those properties are added as properties to the instance of the new object. When these methods are called, the context (the value of `this`) is the current instance.

This is similar to the *Defining function properties as methods on a plain object* recipe in Chapter 6, *Plain Objects*. In that recipe, we overrode methods by direct assignment. By contrast, in this recipe, we are doing this on the prototype. That means that this override applies to every instance of the `InactiveRocket` subclass.

Overriding parent class static methods

We've seen previously that behaviors are not limited to class instances but are also attached to the classes themselves. These `static` methods can also be overridden by subclasses.

In this recipe, we'll see how to override static methods.

Getting ready

This recipe assumes you already have a workspace that allows you to create and run ES modules in your browser. If you don't, please see the first two chapters.

How to do it...

1. Open your command line application and navigate to your workspace.
2. Create a new folder named `08-04-checking-with-instanceof`.
3. Copy or create an `index.html` that loads and runs a `main` function from `main.js`.
4. Create two objects `rocketMap` and `inactiveRocketMap`:

   ```
   // main.js
   let rocketMap = {};
   let inactiveRocketMap = {};
   ```

5. Define a new class named `Rocket`. Add a constructor. Use the name to assign the instance to the `rocketMap` and define a simple `print` method:

   ```
   // main.js
   class Rocket {
     constructor(name) {
       this.name = name;
       rocketMap[name] = this;
       }
     print() {
       console.log(this.name + ' is a rocket');
     }
   }
   ```

6. Add a static `find` method that retrieves an instance from the `rocketMap`:

```
// main.js
class Rocket {
  static find (name) {
    return rocketMap[name];
  }
}
```

7. Create a class named `InactiveRocket` that extends the `Rocket` class and assigns an additional `lastFlow` property in the constructor. Use the `name` to assign the instance to the `inactiveRocketMap` and override the `print` method to include the new property:

```
// main.js
class InactiveRocket extends Rocket {
 constructor(name, lastFlown) {
    super(name);
    this.lastFlown = lastFlown;
    inactiveRocketMap[name] = this;
  }

 print() {
    console.log(this.name + ' is an inactive rocket');
    console.log(`${this.name} was last flown:
    ${this.lastFlown}`);
  }
}
```

8. Add a static `find` method that retrieves an instance from the `rocketMap`:

```
// main.js
class InactiveRocket {
  static find (name) {
    return inactiveRocketMap[name];
  }
}
```

9. Create a `main` function that creates instances of both classes and try to retrieve the instances from the maps:

```
// main.js
export function main() {
  const saturnV = new InactiveRocket('Saturn V');
  const falconHeavy = new Rocket('Falcon Heavy');

  // print rocket for saturn V and falcon heavy
```

```
                console.log('All Rockets:');
                Rocket.find('Saturn V').print();
                Rocket.find('Falcon Heavy').print();
                // print inactive entry for saturn v and attempt falcon
                console.log('Inactive Rockets:');
                InactiveRocket.find('Saturn V').print();
                // throws an error
                InactiveRocket.find('Falcon Heavy').print();
            }
```

10. Start your Python web server and open the following link in your browser: `http://localhost:8000/`.

11. You should see output like the following:

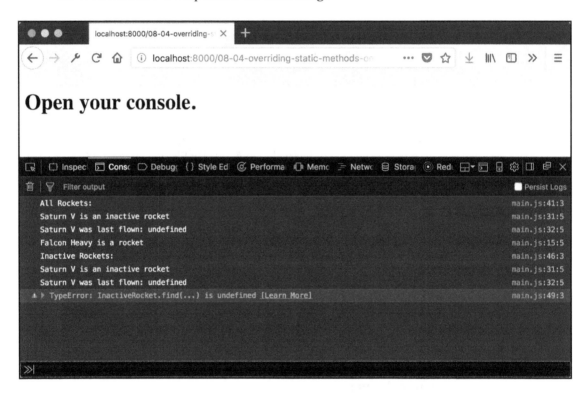

How it works...

Just like the instance methods, static methods defined on the child override those on the parent class. We created the Rocket class with a static method that locates a Rocket instance based on its name. We also created an InactiveRocket class with its own find method that searches in a different map. Because the InactiveRocket class calls super in its constructor, instances of both classes are added to the map used by the Rocket class's find method. While only instances of InactiveRocket are added to the map used in that class's find method.

When we call find on the Rocket class we are able to retrieve instances of both classes. You'll notice that we are unable to locate instances of the base class using the InactiveRocket class's find method.

Calling super methods

Overriding methods is awesome for extending behavior. However, we sometimes want to continue to use behavior from a parent class. This is possible by using the super keyboard to access parent class methods.

In this recipe, we'll see how to use this keyword to access those methods.

Getting ready

This recipe assumes you already have a workspace that allows you to create and run ES modules in your browser. If you don't, please see the first two chapters.

How to do it...

1. Open your command line application and navigate to your workspace.
2. Create a new folder named 08-05-getters-read-only.
3. Copy or create an index.html that loads and runs a main function from main.js.

4. Create a `main.js` file that defines a new class named `Rocket`. Add a constructor that takes a constructor argument `name` and assigns it to an instance property. Then, define a simple `print` method:

```
// main.js
class Rocket {
  constructor(name) {
    this.name = name;
  }

  print() {
    console.log(this.name + ' is a Rocket');
  }
}
```

5. Create a class named `InactiveRocket` that extends the `Rocket` class and assigns an additional `lastFlow` property in the constructor. Then, override the `print` method and call `super.print`:

```
// main.js
class InactiveRocket extends Rocket {
  constructor(name, lastFlown) {
    super(name);
    this.lastFlown = lastFlown;
  }

  print() {
    super.print();
    console.log(`${this.name} was last flown:
    ${this.lastFlown}`);
  }
}
```

6. Create a `main` function that creates instances of both classes and calls their `print` method of both:

```
// main.js
export function main() {
  const saturnV = new InactiveRocket('Saturn V', new Date('May
  14, 1973'));
  const falconHeavy = new Rocket('Falcon Heavy');

  falconHeavy.print();
  saturnV.print();
}
```

7. Start your Python web server and open the following link in your browser: `http://localhost:8000/`.

8. You should see output like the following:

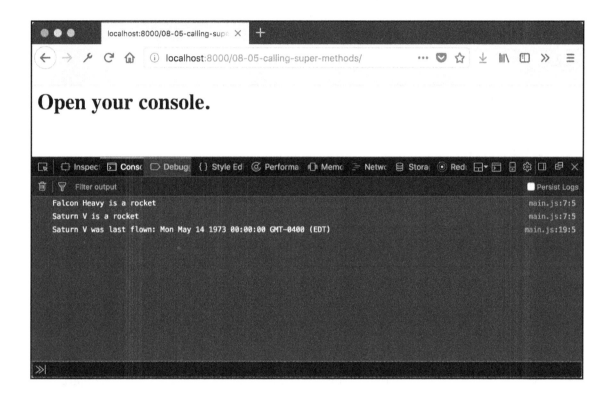

How it works...

Because we overrode the `print` method in the `InactiveRocket` class, calling that method will execute the code defined in that class, rather than the parents. The `super` keyword allows us to reference the prototype of the parent class. So, when the `print` method is called on the `super` keyword, the method as defined on the parent prototype is executed. Thus, we see the output of both `print` methods for the `saturnV` instance.

Using composition rather than inheritance to add behavior

So far, we've seen how to use inheritance to add behavior and compose larger structures. This is not always the ideal approach. In many situations, it's better to use a method known as composition instead. This involves using distinct classes in connection without establishing a hierarchical relationship. The chief advantage here is code clarity and flexibility.

In this recipe, we'll see how to use composition.

Getting ready

This recipe assumes you already have a workspace that allows you to create and run ES modules in your browser. If you don't, please see the first two chapters.

How to do it...

1. Open your command line application and navigate to your workspace.
2. Create a new folder named `08-06-using-composition-instead-of-inherritence`.
3. Copy or create an `index.html` that loads and runs a `main` function from `main.js`.
4. Create a `main.js` file that defines a new class named `Rocket`. Add a constructor that takes a constructor argument `name` and assigns it to an instance property. Then, define a simple `print` method:

```
// main.js
class Rocket {
  constructor(name) {
    this.name = name;
  }

  print() {
    console.log(this.name + ' is a Rocket');
  }
}
```

5. Create a class named `InactiveRocket` that extends the `Rocket` class and assigns an additional `lastFlow` property in the constructor. Then, override the `print` method:

```
// main.js
class InactiveRocket extends Rocket {
 constructor(name, lastFlown) {
    super(name);
    this.lastFlown = lastFlown;
  }

  print() {
    console.log(this.name + ' is an inactive rocket');
    console.log(`${this.name} was last flown:
    ${this.lastFlown}`);
  }
}
```

6. Create a class named `Launcher` that takes a constructor argument `rocket`. Add a method, named `prepareForLaunch`, that aborts if the rocket is inactive:

```
// main.js
class Launcher {
  constructor (rocket) {
    this.rocket = rocket;
  }

  prepareForLaunch () {
    const { rocket } = this;

    if (rocket instanceof InactiveRocket) {
      console.error(`Unable to launch, rocket ${rocket.name}
has
      been inactive since ${rocket.lastFlown}`);
    } else {
      console.log(`${rocket.name} is ready to launch.`);
    }
  }
}
```

7. Create a `main` function that creates two instances of `Launcher`; one for each class of rocket:

```
// main.js
export function main() {
  const saturnV = new InactiveRocket('Saturn V', new Date('May
  14,1973'));
```

```
        const falconHeavy = new Rocket('Falcon Heavy');

        const saturnVLauncher = new Launcher(saturnV);
        const falconHeavyLauncher = new Launcher(falconHeavy);

        saturnVLauncher.prepareForLaunch();
        falconHeavyLauncher.prepareForLaunch();
    }
```

8. Start your Python web server and open the following link in your browser: `http://localhost:8000/`.

9. You should see output like the following:

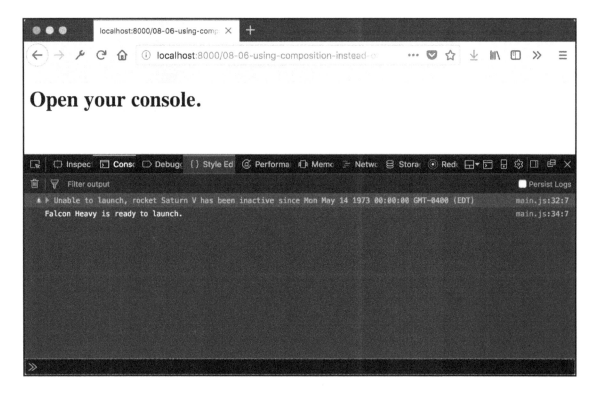

How it works...

In this recipe, we've added an instance of one class (one of the two `Rocket` classes) and used it within the instance of another class (`Launcher`), that isn't related via inheritance. It would be possible to add this launch functionality through a `LaunchableRocket` class, but that would become cumbersome as the kinds of rockets and their relationships change.

In general, adding behaviors through inheritance is constricting; it should be limited to small changes and they should not differ in public interface. The **Dependency Inversion Principle** (**DIP**) is an important concept when considering inheritance.

> Visit the following link to learn more about the DIP: `https://en.wikipedia.org/wiki/Dependency_inversion_principle`.

Using mix-ins to add behavior

We've seen how to use inheritance and composition to add behavior. There is a different method of composition that appends behavior onto existing classes without inheritance. Using mix-ins attaches properties to an object instance at runtime.

In this recipe, we'll see how to use the mix-ins to add shared behavior to classes without inheritance.

Getting ready

This recipe assumes you already have a workspace that allows you to create and run ES modules in your browser. If you don't, please see the first two chapters.

How to do it...

1. Open your command line application and navigate to your workspace.
2. Create a new folder named `08-08-using-mixins`.
3. Copy or create an `index.html` that loads and runs a `main` function from `main.js`.

4. Create a `main.js` file that defines a new class named `Rocket`. In the constructor, extend the current instance with an object named `Launcher`:

```
// main.js
class Rocket {
  constructor(name) {
    Object.assign(this, Launcher);
    this.name = name;
  }
  print() {
    console.log(this.name + ' is a rocket');
  }
}
```

5. Create a class named `InactiveRocket` that extends the `Rocket` class and assigns an additional `lastFlow` property in the constructor:

```
// main.js
class InactiveRocket extends Rocket {
 constructor(name, lastFlown) {
    super(name);
    this.lastFlown = lastFlown;
  }

  print() {
    console.log(this.name + ' is an inactive rocket');
    console.log(`${this.name} was last flown:
    ${this.lastFlown}`);
  }
}
```

6. Create an object named `Launcher` that defines a method named `prepareForLaunch`, which aborts if the rocket is inactive:

```
// main.js
const Launcher = {
  prepareForLaunch () {
    if (this instanceof InactiveRocket) {
      console.error(`Unable to launch, rocket ${this.name} has
      been inactive since ${this.lastFlown}`);
    } else {
      console.log(`${this.name} is ready to launch.`);
    }
  }
}
```

7. Create a `main` function that creates instances of each class of `Rocket` and calls `prepareForLaunch` on each:

```
// main.js

export function main() {
  const saturnV = new InactiveRocket('Saturn V', new Date('May
  14,1973'));
  const falconHeavy = new Rocket('Falcon Heavy');

  saturnV.prepareForLaunch();
  falconHeavy.prepareForLaunch();
}
```

8. Start your Python web server and open the following link in your browser:
`http://localhost:8000/`.

9. You should see output like the following:

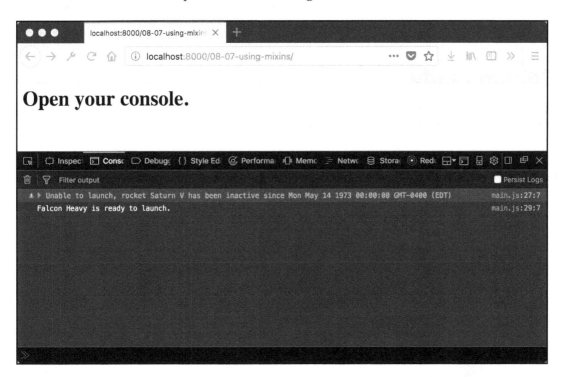

How it works...

`Object.assign` adds all the properties from one object to another. Assigning all of the properties from the `Launcher` onto the new instance makes those available after the object is created. Remember that methods on `this` are simply properties on the prototype with function values. So, adding methods this way is the equivalent of defining these methods on the prototype.

Thus, after applying this mix-in with `Object.assign` we can call methods defined as properties on `Launcher` as instance methods of `Rocket` and `InactiveRocket`.

Passing a class as an argument

Classes, like functions, are first class citizens in JavaScript. This means that they can be returned from functions or passed as arguments. In this recipe, we'll see how to use the latter.

Getting ready

This recipe assumes you already have a workspace that allows you to create and run ES modules in your browser. If you don't, please see the first two chapters.

How to do it...

1. Open your command line application and navigate to your workspace.
2. Create a new folder named `08-08-passing-class-as-an-argument`.
3. Copy or create an `index.html` that loads and runs a `main` function from `main.js`.
4. Create a `main.js` file that defines a new class named `Rocket`:

```
// main.js
class Rocket {
  constructor(name) {
    this.name = name;
  }
}
```

5. Create a class named `InactiveRocket` that extends the `Rocket` class and assigns a `name` and a `lastFlow` property in the constructor:

```
// main.js
class InactiveRocket extends Rocket {
 constructor(name, lastFlown) {
    super();
    this.lastFlown = lastFlown;
 }
}
```

6. Create a function `isA` that takes an instance and a `klass` argument and returns `true` if the constructor is the passed class:

```
// main.js
function isA(instance, klass) {
   return instance.constructor === klass;
}
```

7. Create a `main` function that creates an instance of `InactiveRocket`. Call `isA` to compare the instance against both `Rocket` classes:

```
// main.js
export function main() {
   const saturnV = new InactiveRocket('Saturn V', new Date('May
   14,1973'));

   console.log(saturnV.name + ' instance of Rocket: ' +
   isA(saturnV,Rocket));
   console.log(saturnV.name + ' instance of InactiveRocket: ' +
   isA(saturnV, InactiveRocket));
}
```

8. Start your Python web server and open the following link in your browser: `http://localhost:8000/`.

9. You should see output like the following:

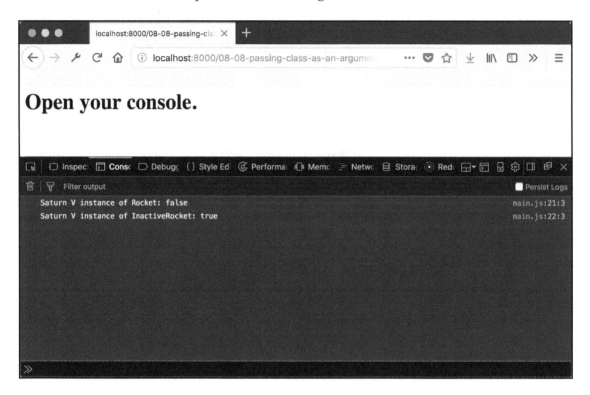

How it works...

The `isA` function compares the identity of the `instance` constructor property against the passed `klass`. This will be `true` if the `instance` argument is an instance of `klass` (in this case we are comparing an instance of the `InactiveRocket` class). It will return `false` for any other class, including `Rocket`.

Because we are comparing the constructor to the class directly, inheritance is not taken into account. If we were to use `instanceOf`, the function would return `true` for `Rocket` as well.

Checking class inheritance with Object.getPrototypeOf

We've seen how to check for inheritance and identity of the instantiated class as a Boolean expression. We might want to also see the full ancestry of an instance at once. In this recipe, we'll see how to do just that.

Getting ready

This recipe assumes you already have a workspace that allows you to create and run ES modules in your browser. If you don't, please see the first two chapters.

How to do it...

1. Open your command line application and navigate to your workspace.
2. Create a new folder named `08-09-checking-class-inheritance`.
3. Copy or create an `index.html` that loads and runs a `main` function from `main.js`.
4. Create a `main.js` file that defines three new `Rocket` classes:

```
// main.js
class Rocket {}
class ActiveRocket extends Rocket {}
class OrbitingRocket extends ActiveRocket {}
```

5. Create a function `listInheritance` that takes an instance and uses `Object.getPrototypeOf` to get the names of all the classes until you reach the null type:

```
// main.js
function listInheritance (instance) {
  const hierarchy = [];
  let currClass = instance.constructor;

  while (currClass.name) {
    hierarchy.push(currClass.name);
    currClass = Object.getPrototypeOf(currClass)
  }

  console.log(hierarchy.join(' -> '));
```

```
    }
```

6. Create a `main` function that creates an instance of `OrbitingRocket` and lists its inheritance:

```javascript
// main.js
export function main() {
  const orbitingRocket = new OrbitingRocket();
  listInheritance(orbitingRocket);
}
```

7. Start your Python web server and open the following link in your browser: `http://localhost:8000/`.

8. You should see output like the following:

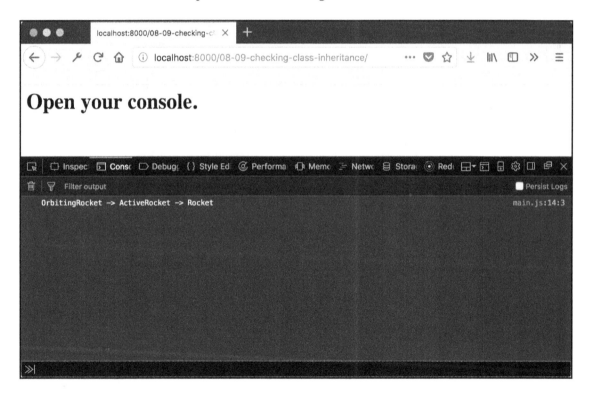

How it works...

All JavaScript prototypes exist in a hierarchy. This means each prototype is extended from another, which in turn extends from another. At the top of the hierarchy is the null type. `Object.getPrototypeOf` traverses up this inheritance tree and climbs its way from the prototype of the instance, all the way to the null type. We can then use the `name` property of each, which will give us the name of that prototype (or class in our case).

Using throw to simulate abstract classes

So far, we've seen how to create and combine classes into a variety of different shapes. Sometimes, however, we want to be able to prevent the creation of a class and only allow instances of extending classes. Other languages provide a facility known as abstract classes. In this recipe, we'll see how to simulate this by throwing errors.

Getting ready

This recipe assumes you already have a workspace that allows you to create and run ES modules in your browser. If you don't, please see the first two chapters.

How to do it...

1. Open your command line application and navigate to your workspace.
2. Create a new folder named `08-10-use-throw-to-simulate-abstract-class`.
3. Copy or create an `index.html` that loads and runs a `main` function from `main.js`.

4. Create a `main.js` file that defines a new class named `Rocket`. In the constructor, check the constructor of the instance, if it's `Rocket`, then throw an error:

```
// main.js
class Rocket {
  constructor (name) {
    this.name = name;
    if (this.constructor === Rocket) {
      throw new Error('Abstract Class Should not be
      instantiated');
    }
  }
}
```

5. Create two child classes of `Rocket`:

```
// main.js
class ActiveRocket extends Rocket {}
class InactiveRocket extends Rocket {}
```

6. Create a `main` function that creates instances of each class of rocket. Notice that the `Rocket` class can't be instantiated:

```
// main.js
export function main() {
  const saturnV = new InactiveRocket('Saturn V');
  console.log(saturnV.name, ' is a Rocket ', saturnV instanceof
  Rocket);

  const falconHeavy = new ActiveRocket('Falcon Heavy');
  console.log(falconHeavy.name, ' is a Rocket ', falconHeavy
  instanceof Rocket);

  // throws an error;
  new Rocket('Not going to make it!');
}
```

7. Start your Python web server and open the following link in your browser: `http://localhost:8000/`.

8. You should see output like the following:

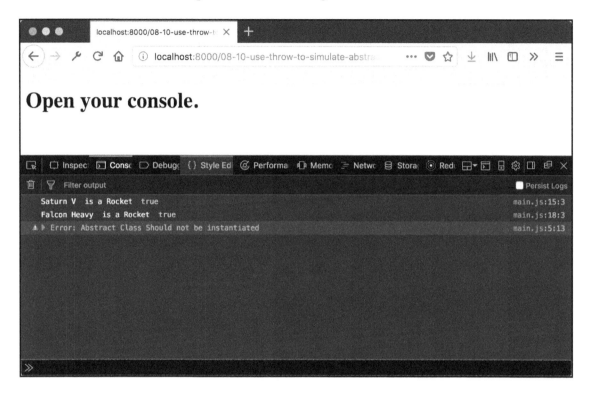

How it works...

The goal of this was to force users of the class to extend the `Rocket` class, rather than instantiate it directly. However, we still want to be able to define behavior in the `base` class. In the constructor of the `Rocket` class you can see how this is done. By comparing the constructor property of the instance with `Rocket` we can see if this has been instantiated directly. If the class is extended, then this comparison will evaluate `false` and the error will not be throw. Thus, we can create `ActiveRocket` and `InactiveRocket` instances.

When creating an instance of `Rocket` directly, the constructor comparison evaluates to `true` and the error is thrown. Thus, we can't create instances of the `Rocket` class, only it's sub-classes.

Larger Structures with Design Patterns

9

In this chapter, we will cover the following recipes:

- Defining steps with template functions
- Assembling customized instances with builders
- Replicating instances with factories
- Processing a structure with the visitor pattern
- Using a singleton to manage instances
- Modifying an existing design pattern to fit different use cases
- Combining existing design patterns to fit different use cases

Introduction

Classes, like objects and functions, are the fundamental building blocks from which we create programs. As programs grow, it becomes more difficult to efficiently and systematically define relationships between entities. When the relationships between data and functionality grow complicated, we can use classes and other objects to organize them. But what do we do when classes and objects proliferate?

Design patterns can be a helpful guide. Useful design patterns are refined from practical implementation. These patterns are intended to solve patterns of a given shape in predictable ways. When properly implemented, they form a contract of expected behaviors. This predictability and regularity (with other implementations of the pattern) assist in reasoning about code and a higher level of abstraction.

In this chapter, we'll see how common design patterns can be used as blueprints for organizing larger structures.

Defining steps with template functions

A template is a design pattern that details the order a given set of operations are to be executed in; however, a template does not outline the steps themselves. This pattern is useful when behavior is divided in to phases that have some conceptual or side effect dependency that requires them to be executed in a specific order.

In this recipe, we'll see how to use the template function design pattern.

Getting ready

This recipe assumes you already have a workspace that allows you to create and run ES modules in your browser. If you don't, please see the first two chapters.

How to do it...

1. Open your command-line application and navigate to your workspace.
2. Create a new folder named `09-01-defining-steps-with-template-functions`.
3. Copy or create an `index.html` file that loads and runs a `main` function from `main.js`.
4. Create a `main.js` file that defines a new abstract `class` named `Mission`:

```
// main.js
class Mission {
  constructor () {
    if (this.constructor === Mission) {
      throw new Error('Mission is an abstract class, must
      extend');
    }
  }
}
```

5. Add a function named `execute` that calls three instance methods—`determineDestination`, `determinPayload`, and `launch`:

```
// main.js
class Mission {
  execute () {
    this.determinDestination();
    this.determinePayload();
    this.launch();
  }
}
```

6. Create a `LunarRover` class that extends the `Mission` class:

```
// main.js
class LunarRover extends Mission {}
```

7. Add a constructor that assigns `name` to an instance property:

```
// main.js
class LunarRover extends Mission
  constructor (name) {
    super();
    this.name = name;
  }
}
```

8. Implement the three methods called by `Mission.execute`:

```
// main.js
class LunarRover extends Mission {}
  determinDestination() {
    this.destination = 'Oceanus Procellarum';
  }

  determinePayload() {
    this.payload = 'Rover with camera and mass spectrometer.';
  }

  launch() {
    console.log(`
Destination: ${this.destination}
Playload: ${this.payload}
Lauched!
Rover Will arrive in a week.
    `);
  }
```

```
            }
```

9. Create a `JovianOrbiter` class that also extends the `Mission` class:

```
// main.js
class LunarRover extends Mission {}
constructor (name) {
    super();
    this.name = name;
}

  determinDestination() {
    this.destination = 'Jovian Orbit';
  }

  determinePayload() {
    this.payload = 'Orbiter with decent module.';
  }

  launch() {
    console.log(`
Destination: ${this.destination}
Playload: ${this.payload}
Lauched!
Orbiter Will arrive in 7 years.
    `);
  }
}
```

10. Create a `main` function that creates both concrete mission types and executes them:

```
// main.js
export function main() {
  const jadeRabbit = new LunarRover('Jade Rabbit');
  jadeRabbit.execute();
  const galileo = new JovianOrbiter('Galileo');
  galileo.execute();
}
```

11. Start your Python web server and open the following link in your browser: `http://localhost:8000/`.

12. The output should appear as follows:

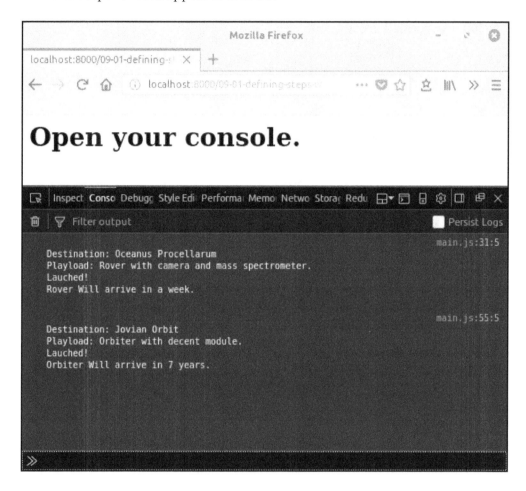

How it works...

The `Mission` abstract class defines the `execute` method, which calls the other instance methods in a particular order. You'll notice that the methods called are not defined by the `Mission` class. This implementation detail is the responsibility of the extending classes. This use of abstract classes allows child classes to be used by code that takes advantage of the interface defined by the abstract class.

In the template function pattern, it is the responsibility of the child classes to define the steps. When they are instantiated, and the `execute` method is called, those steps are then performed in the specified order.

Ideally, we'd be able to ensure that `Mission.execute` was not overridden by any inheriting classes. Overriding this method works against the pattern and breaks the contract associated with it.

This pattern is useful for organizing data-processing pipelines. The guarantee that these steps will occur in a given order means that, if side effects are eliminated, the instances can be organized more flexibly. The implementing class can then organize these steps in the best possible way.

Assembling customized instances with builders

The previous recipe shows how to organize the operations of a class. Sometimes, object initialization can also be complicated. In these situations, it can be useful to take advantage of another design pattern: builders.

In this recipe, we'll see how to use builders to organize the initialization of more complicated objects.

Getting ready

This recipe assumes you already have a workspace that allows you to create and run ES modules in your browser. If you don't, please see the first two chapters.

How to do it...

1. Open your command-line application and navigate to your workspace.
2. Create a new folder named `09-02-assembling-instances-with-builders`.

3. Create a `main.js` file that defines a new `class` named `Mission`, which that takes a `name` constructor argument and assigns it to an instance property. Also, create a `describe` method that prints out some details:

```js
// main.js
class Mission {
  constructor (name) {
    this.name = name;
  }

  describe () {
    console.log(`
      The ${this.name} mission will be launched by a
        ${this.rocket.name}
      rocket, and deliver a ${this.payload.name} to
      ${this.destination.name}.
    `);
  }
}
```

4. Create classes named `Destination`, `Payload`, and `Rocket`, which receive a `name` property as a constructor parameter and assign it to an instance property:

```js
// main.js

class Destination {
  constructor (name) {
    this.name = name;
  }
}

class Payload {
  constructor (name) {
    this.name = name;
  }
}

class Rocket {
  constructor (name) {
    this.name = name;
  }
}
```

5. Create a `MissionBuilder` class that defines the `setMissionName`, `setDestination`, `setPayload`, and `setRocket` methods:

```
// main.js
class MissionBuilder {

  setMissionName (name) {
    this.missionName = name;
    return this;
  }

  setDestination (destination) {
    this.destination = destination;
    return this;
  }

  setPayload (payload) {
    this.payload = payload;
    return this;
  }

  setRocket (rocket) {
    this.rocket = rocket;
    return this;
  }
}
```

6. Create a `build` method that creates a new `Mission` instance with the appropriate properties:

```
// main.js
class MissionBuilder {
  build () {
    const mission = new Mission(this.missionName);
    mission.rocket = this.rocket;
    mission.destination = this.destination;
    mission.payload = this.payload;
    return mission;
  }
}
```

7. Create a `main` function that uses `MissionBuilder` to create a new mission instance:

```
// main.js
export function main() {
  // build an describe a mission
```

```
new MissionBuilder()
    .setMissionName('Jade Rabbit')
    .setDestination(new Destination('Oceanus Procellarum'))
    .setPayload(new Payload('Lunar Rover'))
    .setRocket(new Rocket('Long March 3B Y-23'))
    .build()
    .describe();
}
```

8. Start your Python web server and open the following link in your browser: `http://localhost:8000/`.

9. Your output should appear as follows:

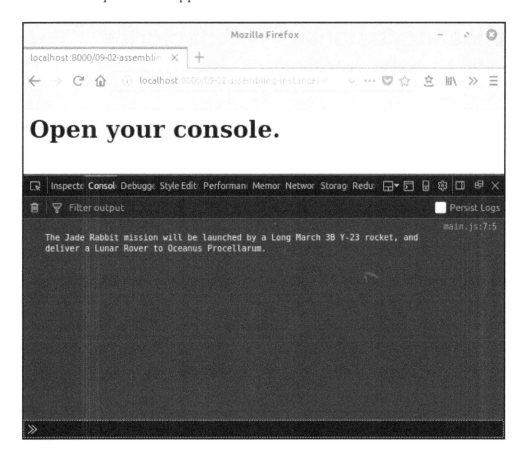

How it works...

The builder defines methods for assigning all the relevant properties and defines a build method that ensures that each is called and assigned appropriately. Builders are like template functions, but instead of ensuring that a set of operations are executed in the correct order, they ensure that an instance is properly configured before returning.

Because each instance method of `MissionBuilder` returns the `this` reference, the methods can be chained. The last line of the `main` function calls `describe` on the new `Mission` instance that is returned from the `build` method.

Replicating instances with factories

Like builders, factories are a way of organizing object construction. They differ from builders in how they are organized. Often, the interface of factories is a single function call. This makes factories easier to use, if less customizable, than builders.

In this recipe, we'll see how to use factories to easily replicate instances.

Getting ready

This recipe assumes you already have a workspace that allows you to create and run ES modules in your browser. If you don't, please see the first two chapters.

How to do it...

1. Open your command-line application and navigate to your workspace.
2. Create a new folder named `09-03-replicating-instances-with-factories`.
3. Copy or create an `index.html` that loads and runs a `main` function from `main.js`.

4. Create a `main.js` file that defines a new `class` named `Mission`. Add a constructor that takes a `name` constructor argument and assigns it to an instance property. Also, define a simple `describe` method:

```
// main.js
class Mission {
  constructor (name) {
    this.name = name;
  }

  describe () {
    console.log(`
The ${this.name} mission will be launched by a
${this.rocket.name} rocket, and
deliver a ${this.payload.name} to ${this.destination.name}.
    `);
  }
}
```

5. Create three classes named `Destination`, `Payload`, and `Rocket`, that take `name` as a constructor argument and assign it to an instance property:

```
// main.js
class Destination {
  constructor (name) {
    this.name = name;
  }
}

class Payload {
  constructor (name) {
    this.name = name;
  }
}

class Rocket {
  constructor (name) {
    this.name = name;
  }
}
```

6. Create a `MarsMissionFactory` object with a single `create` method that takes two arguments: `name` and `rocket`. This method should create a new `Mission` using those arguments:

```
// main.js

const MarsMissionFactory = {
  create (name, rocket) {
    const mission = new Mission(name);
    mission.destination = new Destination('Martian surface');
    mission.payload = new Payload('Mars rover');
    mission.rocket = rocket;
    return mission;
  }
}
```

7. Create a `main` method that creates and describes two similar missions:

```
// main.js

export function main() {
  // build an describe a mission
  MarsMissionFactory
    .create('Curiosity', new Rocket('Atlas V'))
    .describe();
  MarsMissionFactory
    .create('Spirit', new Rocket('Delta II'))
    .describe();
}
```

8. Start your Python web server and open the following link in your browser: `http://localhost:8000/`.

9. Your output should appear as follows:

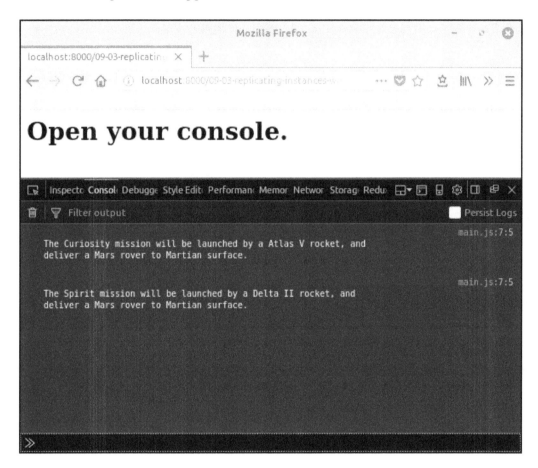

How it works...

The `create` method takes a subset of the properties needed to create a new mission. The remaining values are provided by the method itself. This allows factories to simplify the process of creating similar instances. In the `main` function, you can see that two Mars missions have been created, only differing in name and `Rocket` instance. We've halved the number of values needed to create an instance.

This pattern can help reduce instantiation logic. In this recipe, we simplified the creation of different kinds of missions by identifying the common attributes, encapsulating those in the body of the factory function, and using arguments to supply the remaining properties. In this way, commonly used instance shapes can be created without additional boilerplate code.

Processing a structure with the visitor pattern

The patterns we've seen thus far organize the construction of objects and the execution of operations. The next pattern we'll look at is specially made to traverse and perform operations on hierarchical structures.

In this recipe, we'll be looking at the visitor pattern.

Getting ready

This recipe assumes you already have a workspace that allows you to create and run ES modules in your browser. If you don't, please see the first two chapters.

Additionally, this recipe assumes that you've completed the previous recipe, *Assembling customized instances with builders*. If not, complete that recipe first.

How to do it...

1. Open your command-line application and navigate to your workspace.
2. Copy the `09-02-assembling-instances-with-builders` folder to a new `09-04-processing-a-structure-with-the-visitor-pattern` directory.

3. Add a class named `MissionInspector` to `main.js`. Create a `visitor` method that calls a corresponding method for each of the following types: `Mission`, `Destination`, `Rocket`, and `Payload`:

    ```
    // main.js
    /* visitor that inspects mission */
    class MissionInspector {
    ```

```
    visit (element) {
      if (element instanceof Mission) {
        this.visitMission(element);
      }
      else if (element instanceof Destination) {
        this.visitDestination(element);
      }
      else if (element instanceof Rocket) {
        this.visitRocket(element);
      }
      else if (element instanceof Payload) {
        this.visitPayload(element);
      }
    }
  }
```

4. Create a `visitMission` method that logs out an `ok` message:

```
// main.js
class MissionInspector {
  visitMission (mission) {
    console.log('Mission ok');
    mission.describe();
      }
  }
```

5. Create a `visitDestination` method that throws an error if the destination is not in an approved list:

```
// main.js
class MissionInspector {
  visitDestination (destination) {
    const name = destination.name.toLowerCase();

    if (
      name === 'mercury' ||
      name === 'venus' ||
      name === 'earth' ||
      name === 'moon' ||
      name === 'mars'
    ) {
      console.log('Destination: ', name, ' approved');
    } else {
      throw new Error('Destination: '' + name + '' not approved
      at this time');
    }
      }
```

```
        }
```

6. Create a `visitPayload` method that throws an error if the `payload` isn't valid:

```js
// main.js
class MissionInspector {
  visitPayload (payload) {
    const name = payload.name.toLowerCase();
    const payloadExpr = /(orbiter)|(rover)/;

    if ( payloadExpr.test(name) ) {
      console.log('Payload: ', name, ' approved');
    }
    else {
      throw new Error('Payload: '' + name + '' not approved at
      this time');
    }
  }
}
```

7. Create a `visitRocket` method that logs out an `ok` message:

```js
// main.js
class MissionInspector {

  visitRocket (rocket) {
    console.log('Rocket: ', rocket.name, ' approved');
  }
}
```

8. Add an `accept` method to the `Mission` class that calls `accept` on its constituents, then tells `visitor` to visit the current instance:

```js
// main.js
class Mission {

  // other mission code ...

  accept (visitor) {
    this.rocket.accept(visitor);
    this.payload.accept(visitor);
    this.destination.accept(visitor);
    visitor.visit(this);
  }
}
```

9. Add an `accept` method to the `Destination` class that tells `visitor` to visit the current instance:

```
// main.js
class Destination {

  // other mission code ...


  accept (visitor) {
    visitor.visit(this);
    }
  }
```

10. Add an `accept` method to the `Payload` class that tells `visitor` to visit the current instance:

```
// main.js
class Payload {

  // other mission code ...

  accept (visitor) {
    visitor.visit(this);
    }
  }
```

11. Add an `accept` method to the `Rocket` class that tells `visitor` to visit the current instance:

```
// main.js
class Rocket {

  // other mission code ...

  accept (visitor) {
    visitor.visit(this);
    }
  }
```

12. Create a `main` function that creates different instances with the builder, visits them with the `MissionInspector` instance, and logs out any thrown errors:

```
// main.js
export function main() {
  // build an describe a mission
```

```
const jadeRabbit = new MissionBuilder()
  .setMissionName('Jade Rabbit')
  .setDestination(new Destination('Moon'))
  .setPayload(new Payload('Lunar Rover'))
  .setRocket(new Rocket('Long March 3B Y-23'))
  .build();

const curiosity = new MissionBuilder()
  .setMissionName('Curiosity')
  .setDestination(new Destination('Mars'))
  .setPayload(new Payload('Mars Rover'))
  .setRocket(new Rocket('Delta II'))
  .build();

// expect error from Destination
const buzz = new MissionBuilder()
  .setMissionName('Buzz Lightyear')
  .setDestination(new Destination('Too Infinity And Beyond'))
  .setPayload(new Payload('Interstellar Orbiter'))
  .setRocket(new Rocket('Self Propelled'))
  .build();

// expect error from payload
const terraformer = new MissionBuilder()
  .setMissionName('Mars Terraformer')
  .setDestination(new Destination('Mars'))
  .setPayload(new Payload('Terraformer'))
  .setRocket(new Rocket('Light Sail'))
  .build();

const inspector = new MissionInspector();

[jadeRabbit, curiosity, buzz, terraformer].forEach((mission)
=>
  {
  try {
    mission.accept(inspector);
  } catch (e) { console.error(e); }
});
}
```

13. Start your Python web server and open the following link in your browser: `http://localhost:8000/`.

14. Your output should appear as follows:

How it works...

The visitor pattern has two components. The visitor processes the subject objects and the subjects tell other related subjects about the visitor, and when the current subject should be visited.

The `accept` method is required for each subject to receive a notification that there is a visitor. That method then makes two types of method call. The first is the `accept` method on its related subjects. The second is the `visitor` method on the visitor. In this way, the visitor traverses a structure by being passed around by the subjects.

The `visitor` methods are used to process different types of node. In some languages, this is handled by language-level **polymorphism**. In JavaScript, we can use run-time type checks to do this.

The visitor pattern is a good option for processing hierarchical structures of objects, where the structure is not known ahead of time, but the types of subjects are known.

Using a singleton to manage instances

Sometimes, there are objects that are resource intensive. They may require time, memory, battery power, or network usage that are unavailable or inconvenient. It is often useful to manage the creation and sharing of instances.

In this recipe, we'll see how to use singletons to manage instances.

Getting ready

This recipe assumes you already have a workspace that allows you to create and run ES modules in your browser. If you don't, please see the first two chapters.

How to do it...

1. Open your command-line application and navigate to your workspace.
2. Create a new folder named `09-05-singleton-to-manage-instances`.
3. Copy or create an `index.html` that loads and runs a `main` function from `main.js`.

4. Create a `main.js` file that defines a new `class` named `Rocket`. Add a constructor takes a `name` constructor argument and assigns it to an instance property:

```
// main.js
class Rocket {
  constructor (name) {
    this.name = name;
  }
}
```

5. Create a `RocketManager` object that has a `rockets` property. Add a `findOrCreate` method that indexes `Rocket` instances by the `name` property:

```
// main.js
const RocketManager = {
  rockets: {},
  findOrCreate (name) {
    const rocket = this.rockets[name] || new Rocket(name);
    this.rockets[name] = rocket;
    return rocket;
  }
}
```

6. Create a `main` function that creates instances with and without the manager. Compare the instances and see whether they are identical:

```
// main.js
export function main() {
  const atlas = RocketManager.findOrCreate('Atlas V');
  const atlasCopy = RocketManager.findOrCreate('Atlas V');
  const atlasClone = new Rocket('Atlas V');

  console.log('Copy is the same: ', atlas === atlasCopy);
  console.log('Clone is the same: ', atlas === atlasClone);
}
```

7. Start your Python web server and open the following link in your browser:
`http://localhost:8000/`.

8. Your output should appear as follows:

How it works...

The object stores references to the instances, indexed by the string value given with `name`. This map is created when the module loads, so it is persisted through the life of the program. The singleton is then able to look up the object and returns instances created by `findOrCreate` with the same name.

Conserving resources and simplifying communication are primary motivations for using singletons. Creating a single object for multiple uses is more efficient in terms of space and time needed than creating several. Plus, having single instances for messages to be communicated through makes communication between different parts of a program easier.

Singletons may require more sophisticated indexing if they are relying on more complicated data.

Modifying an existing design pattern to fit different use cases

Patterns are not commandments received from a higher plane. They have their origins in, and have been refined from, real-world engineering projects. Patterns can be modified to fit new situations better.

In this recipe, we'll see how to modify the factory pattern to make creating missions easier.

Getting ready

This recipe assumes you already have a workspace that allows you to create and run ES modules in your browser. If you don't, please see the first two chapters.

How to do it...

1. Open your command-line application and navigate to your workspace.
2. Create a new folder named `09-06-modifying-existing-design-pattern-to-fit-differet-use-cases`.
3. Copy or create an `index.html` that loads and runs a `main` function from `main.js`.
4. Create a `main.js` file that defines a new `class` named `Mission`. Add a constructor that takes a `name` constructor argument and assigns it to an instance property. Also, define a simple `print` method:

```js
// main.js
class Mission {
  constructor (name) {
    this.name = name;
  }

  describe () {
    console.log(` The ${this.name} mission will be launched by a
    ${this.rocket.name}, and deliver a ${this.payload.name} to
    ${this.destination.name}.
    `);
  }
}
```

5. Create a class named `Destination`. Add a constructor takes a name constructor takes a `name` constructor argument and assigns it to an instance property:

```
// main.js
class Destination {
  constructor (name) {
    this.name = name;
  }
}
```

6. Create a class named `Payload`. Add a constructor that takes a `name` constructor argument and assigns it to an instance property:

```
// main.js
class Payload {
  constructor (name) {
    this.name = name;
  }
}
```

7. Create a class named `Rocket`. Add a constructor that takes a `name` constructor argument and assigns it to an instance property:

```
// main.js
class Rocket {
  constructor (name) {
    this.name = name;
  }
}
```

8. Create a function named `MissionProgramFactoryFn` that takes `rocketName`, `destinationName`, and `payloadName` arguments. This function should return a function that receives a `name` argument and returns a new `mission` with all of the properties:

```
// main.js

function MissionProgramFactoryFn(rocketName, destinationName,
payloadName) {
  return (name) => {
    const mission = new Mission(name);
    mission.rocket = new Rocket(rocketName);
    mission.destination = new Destination(destinationName);
    mission.payload = new Payload(payloadName);
    return mission;
  }
}
```

9. Create a `main` function that creates two program factories. Create and describe multiple missions with the instances:

```
// main.js
export function main() {
  const marsRoverProgram = MissionProgramFactoryFn('AtlasV',
  'MartianSurface', 'Mars Rover');
  marsRoverProgram('Curiosity').describe();
  marsRoverProgram('Spirit').describe();

  const interstellarProgram = MissionProgramFactoryFn('Warp
  Drive',
  'Vulcan', 'Dimplomatic Vessal');
  interstellarProgram('Enterprise E').describe();
  interstellarProgram('Defiant').describe();
}
```

10. Start your Python web server and open the following link in your browser: `http://localhost:8000/`.

11. Your output should appear as follows:

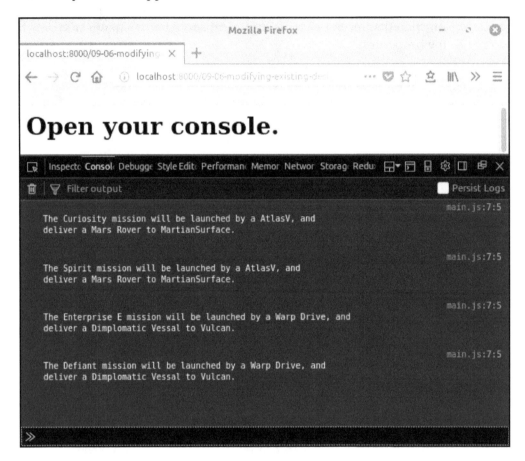

How it works...

In the preceding example, we modified the factory pattern to be a bit more flexible. Rather than calling the factory function directly, we created new ones with the MissionProgramFactoryFn function. In effect, we created a factory of factories!

Variables within a JavaScript function are available to any blocks contained by that function. Thus, the rocketName, destinationName, and payloadName values are available to the body of the factory functions returned from MissionProgramFactoryFn. This way, we reuse common values for new instances without repeating them.

Returning a function from a function is called a second-order function; this pattern is common in JavaScript.

Combining existing design patterns to fit different use cases

Modifying and extending patterns doesn't mean that we must forge ahead into *terra incognita*. It is still advisable to use well-known patterns when tackling new problems.

In this recipe, we'll see how to combine two patterns to better fit a given use case.

Getting ready

This recipe assumes you already have a workspace that allows you to create and run ES modules in your browser. If you don't, please see the first two chapters.

How to do it...

1. Open your command-line application and navigate to your workspace.
2. Create a new folder named `09-07-combine-design-patters-to-fit-new-use-case`.
3. Copy or create an `index.html` that loads and runs a `main` function from `main.js`.
4. Create a `main.js` file that defines a new `class` named `Mission`. Create a constructor that assigns a `name` argument to an instance variable. Add a simple `print` function:

```
// main.js
class Mission {
  constructor (name) {
    this.name = name;
  }

  describe () {
    console.log(`
The ${this.name} mission will be launched by a
${this.rocket.name} rocket, and
```

```
      deliver a ${this.payload.name} to ${this.destination.name}.
        `);
    }
  }
```

5. Create a class named `Destination`. Create a constructor that assigns a `name` argument to an instance variable:

```
// main.js
class Destination {
  constructor (name) {
    this.name = name;
  }
}
```

6. Create a class named `Payload`. Create a constructor that assigns a `name` argument to an instance variable:

```
// main.js
class Payload {
  constructor (name) {
    this.name = name;
  }
}
```

7. Create a class named `Rocket`. Create a constructor that assigns a `name` argument to an instance variable:

```
// main.js
class Rocket {
  constructor (name) {
    this.name = name;
  }
}
```

8. Create a `MissionBuilder` class that defines setters for the mission's `name`, `payload`, and `rocket` properties:

```
// main.js
class MissionBuilder {
  setMissionName (name) {
    this.missionName = name;
    return this;
  }

  setDestination (destination) {
    this.destination = destination;
```

```
      return this;
    }

    setPayload (payload) {
      this.payload = payload;
      return this;
    }

    setRocket (rocket) {
      this.rocket = rocket;
      return this;
    }
}
```

9. Add a `build` function that assembles all of these properties:

```
// main.js
class MissionBuilder {
  build () {
    const mission = new Mission(this.missionName);
    mission.rocket = this.rocket;
    mission.destination = this.destination;
    mission.payload = this.payload;
    return mission;
  }
}
```

10. Create a `MarsMissionFactory` object that takes `name` and `rocket` arguments, and uses `MissionBuilder` to assemble a new mission:

```
// main.js

const MarsMissionFactory = {
  create (name, rocket) {
    return new MissionBuilder()
      .setMissionName(name)
      .setDestination(new Destination('Martian Surface'))
      .setPayload(new Payload('Mars Rover'))
      .setRocket(rocket)
      .build()
  }
}
```

11. Create a `main` function that creates and describes a few instances of Mars missions:

```
// main.js
export function main() {
  // build an describe a mission
  MarsMissionFactory
    .create('Curiosity', new Rocket('Atlas V'))
    .describe();
  MarsMissionFactory
    .create('Spirit', new Rocket('Delta II'))
    .describe();
}
```

12. Start your Python web server and open the following link in your browser: `http://localhost:8000/`.

13. Your output should appear as follows:

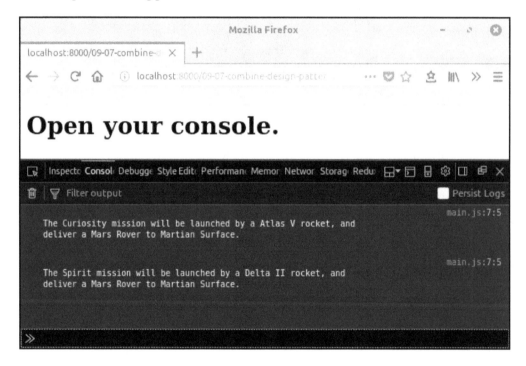

How it works...

`MarsMissionFactory` receives the values for the `name` and `rocket` properties of `mission`, then supplies the remaining values to a builder instance. This narrows the properties required to make a new `mission`, while still using the builder interface.

This method of combining rather than modifying patterns is preferable in many use cases. Like more established library code, better-known patterns have better-defined contracts and more predictable behavior than custom ones. Their familiarity makes them easier for a newcomer to understand.

10
Working with Arrays

In this chapter, we will cover the following recipes:

- Using Array#find and Array#filter to find values in an array
- Using Array#slice to get a subset of an array
- Using Array#every and Array#some to test array values
- Using Array.map to produce values
- Using Array.reduce to transform data
- Extracting array members with destructuring
- Getting the head and tail of array using the rest operator
- Combining arrays with the spread operator

Introduction

Arrays are a fundamental data structure in almost every language, and JavaScript is no exception. Common tasks for these collections include, among others, searching, dividing, and combining them. Until recently, this meant writing a lot of loops, or including large libraries that implemented these loops. ES6, however, includes additions to the Array API that make these tasks much easier.

Using Array#find and Array#filter to find values in an array

When searching for items in an array, sometimes we search for a single item, other times we search for multiple items that mean some criteria. The Array#find and Array#filter functions are intended to simplify this.

In this recipe, we'll take a look at how to use these two functions to locate elements within an array.

Getting ready

This recipe assumes that you already have a workspace that allows you to create and run ES modules in your browser. If you don't, refer to the first two chapters.

How to do it...

1. Open your command-line application, and navigate to your workspace.
2. Create a new folder named `10-01-using-find-and-filter`.
3. Copy or create an `index.html` that loads and runs a `main` function from `main.js`.
4. Create a `main.js` file that defines a new abstract `class` named `Rocket`. Assign a `name` instance property upon construction:

```
// main.js
class Rocket {
  constructor(name) {
    this.name = name;
  }
}
```

5. Create a `main` function that constructs several `Rocket` instances:

```
// main.js
export function main() {
  const saturnV = new Rocket('US: Saturn V');
  const falconHeavy = new Rocket('US: Falcon Heavy');
  const longMarch = new Rocket('CN: Long March');
  const rockets = [saturnV, falconHeavy, longMarch];
}
```

6. Use the `find` method to locate the first American `Rocket`:

```
// main.js
export function main () {
  // ...
  const firstUSRocket = rockets.find((rocket) =>
  rocket.name.indexOf('US') === 0);
  console.log('First US Rocket: ', firstUSRocket.name);
}
```

7. Use the `filter` method to find all `American Rockets` instances:

```
// main.js
export function main () {
  // ...
  const allUSRockets = rockets.filter((rocket) =>
  rocket.name.indexOf('US') === 0);
  console.log('All US Rockets: ',allUSRockets);
}
```

8. Start your Python web server and open the following link in your browser:
`http://localhost:8000/`.

9. You will see output displayed as follows:

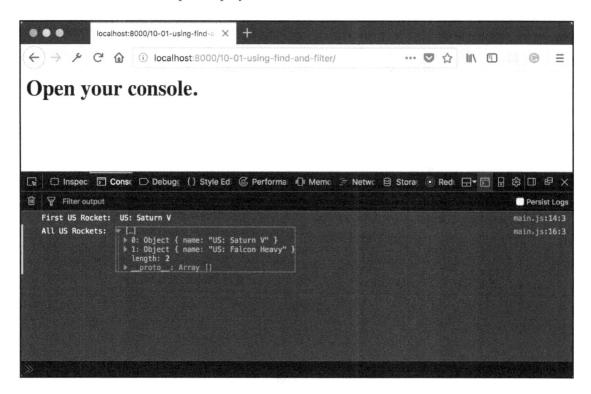

How it works...

Both the `find` and `filter` methods take a function that has a single parameter (an item from the array) and returns a Boolean value. If the function returns `true`, then the current item is a match. If it returns false, then it is not. The `find` method terminates after the first match and returns that value. The `filter` method creates a new array from all matches from the current array.

In the above recipe, we see that the `find` method returns the first `Rocket` identified as American, while the `filter` method returns all of the `rockets` that are identified as American.

Using Array#slice to get a subset of the array

Sometimes, we want a subset of an array based on the array indices rather than on the contents of the array at those indices. In this recipe, we'll take a look at how to use slice to get a subset of an array.

Getting ready

This recipe assumes that you already have a workspace that allows you to create and run ES modules in your browser. If you don't, refer to the first two chapters.

How to do it...

1. Open your command-line application, and navigate to your workspace.
2. Create a new folder named `10-02-using-slice-to-get-subset`.
3. Create a `main.js` file that defines a new `class` named `Rocket` that takes a constructor argument `name` and assigns it to an instance property:

```
// main.js
class Rocket {
  constructor(name) {
    this.name = name;
  }
}
```

4. Create a `main` function that creates several `Rocket` instances and places them into an array:

```
// main.js
export function main() {
  const saturnV = new Rocket('US: Saturn V');
  const falconHeavy = new Rocket('US: Falcon Heavy');
  const soyuz = new Rocket('USSR: Soyuz');
  const dongFeng = new Rocket('CN: Dong Feng');
  const longMarch = new Rocket('CN: Long March');
  const rockets = [saturnV, falconHeavy, soyuz, dongFeng,
  longMarch];
}
```

5. Divide the `Rockets` array into three subsets based on the country:

```
// main.js
export function main() {
  //....
  const americanRockets = rockets.slice(0, 2);
  const sovietRockets = rockets.slice(2, 3);
  const chineseRockets = rockets.slice(3, 5);
  console.log('American Rockets: ', americanRockets);
  console.log('Soviet Rockets: ', sovietRockets);
  console.log('Chinese Rockets: ', chineseRockets);
}
```

6. Start your Python web server and open the following link in your browser: `http://localhost:8000/`.

7. You should see the following output:

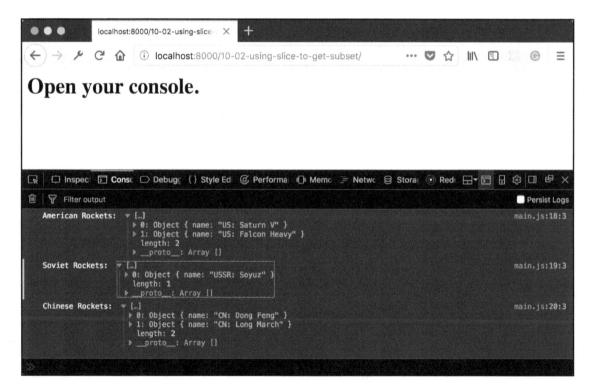

How it works...

The **slice** method takes two parameters, a start index and an end index. The end index is noninclusive. This means that the new set will include the elements between the start and end index, including the element at the start index, but not the element at the end index.

This might seem a bit confusing, but think of it this way. Consider that the start index is 2 and the end index is 3. The difference between those two numbers is 1, and there is a single element in the resulting subset. For indices 0 and 2, the difference is 2 and there will be two elements in the resulting subset.

Using Array#every and Array#some to test array values

Sometimes, we need to know information about the array as a whole rather than individual elements, such as "Are there any elements that meet some criterion?" or "Do all the elements meet some criterion?".

In this recipe, we'll take a look at how to use the `some` and `every` methods to test an array.

Getting ready

This recipe assumes that you already have a workspace that allows you to create and run ES modules in your browser. If you don't, refer to the first two chapters.

How to do it...

1. Open your command-line application, and navigate to your workspace.
2. Create a new folder named `10-03-using-every-and-some-to-test-values`.

3. Create a `main.js` file that defines a new `class` named `Rocket` that takes a constructor argument `name` and assigns it to an instance property:

```
// main.js
class Rocket {
  constructor(name) {
    this.name = name;
  }
}
```

4. Create a `main` function that creates several `Rocket` instances and places them into an array:

```
// main.js
export function main() {
  const saturnV = new Rocket('US: Saturn V');
  const falconHeavy = new Rocket('US: Falcon Heavy');
  const soyuz = new Rocket('USSR: Soyuz');
  const dongFeng = new Rocket('CN: Dong Feng');
  const longMarch = new Rocket('CN: Long March');
  const rockets = [saturnV, falconHeavy, soyuz, dongFeng,
  longMarch];
}
```

5. Use the `every` method to determine whether all of the members are instances of the `Rocket` class:

```
// main.js
export function main() {
  //...
  const allAreRockets = rockets.every((rocket) => rocket
  instanceof Rocket);
  console.log('All are Rockets: ', allAreRockets)
}
```

6. Use the `every` method to determine whether all of the members are `American` `Rockets`:

```
// main.js
export function main() {
  //...
  const allAmerican = rockets.every((rocket) =>
  rocket.name.indexOf('US:') === 0);
  console.log('All rockets are American: ', allAmerican);
}
```

7. Use the `some` method to determine whether any of the members are `American Rockets`:

```
// main.js
export function main() {
  //...
  const someAmerican = rockets.some((rocket) =>
  rocket.name.indexOf('US:') === 0);
  console.log('Some rockets are American: ', someAmerican);
}
```

8. Start your Python web server and open the following link in your browser: `http://localhost:8000/`.

9. You should see the following output:

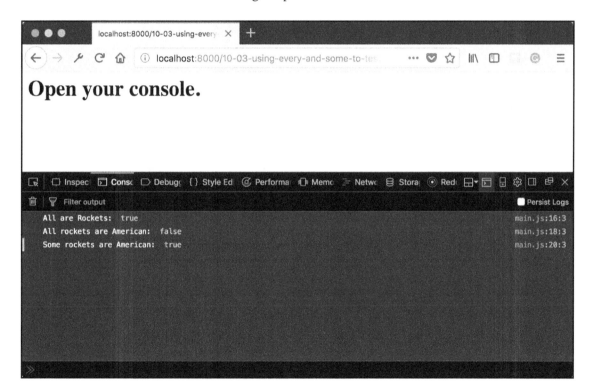

How it works...

The `every` and `some` methods work similarly to the `filter` and `find` methods. They take a function, which receives an array element as a parameter, and return a Boolean. The truth value of this Boolean is used by the `every` and `some` methods to reduce to a single value. The `some` method returns true as soon as any of the callbacks return `true`. The `every` method visits all the elements and only returns `true` if all of the callbacks return `true`.

Using Array.map to produce values

Other array operations are intended to produce new values. This can be a property from array elements or any other value calculated for each. The `map` method visits each element and collects the values into a new array.

In this recipe, we'll take a look at how to use `map` to create an array of new values.

Getting ready

This recipe assumes that you already have a workspace that allows you to create and run ES modules in your browser. If you don't, refer to the first two chapters.

How to do it...

1. Open your command-line application, and navigate to your workspace.
2. Create a new folder named `10-04-map-to-produce-values`.
3. Create a `main.js` file that defines a new `class` named `Rocket` that takes a constructor argument `name` and assigns it to an instance property:

```
// main.js
class Rocket {
  constructor(name) {
    this.name = name;
  }
  }
```

4. Create a `main` function that creates several `Rocket` instances and places them into an array:

```
// main.js
export function main() {
  const saturnV = new Rocket('US: Saturn V');
  const falconHeavy = new Rocket('US: Falcon Heavy');
  const soyuz = new Rocket('USSR: Soyuz');
  const dongFeng = new Rocket('CN: Dong Feng');
  const longMarch = new Rocket('CN: Long March');
  const rockets = [saturnV, falconHeavy, soyuz, dongFeng,
  longMarch];
}
```

5. Use the `map` method, and return a string representation of each element's nationality:

```
// main.js
export function main() {
  //...
  const nationalities = rockets.map((rocket) => {
    if (rocket.name.indexOf('USSR:') === 0) {
      return 'Soviet';
    }
    if (rocket.name.indexOf('CN:') === 0) {
      return 'Chinese';
    }
    if (rocket.name.indexOf('US:') === 0) {
      return 'American';
    }

    return 'unknown';
  });

  console.log('Nationalities:', nationalities)
}
```

6. Start your Python web server and open the following link in your browser: `http://localhost:8000/`.

7. You should see the following output:

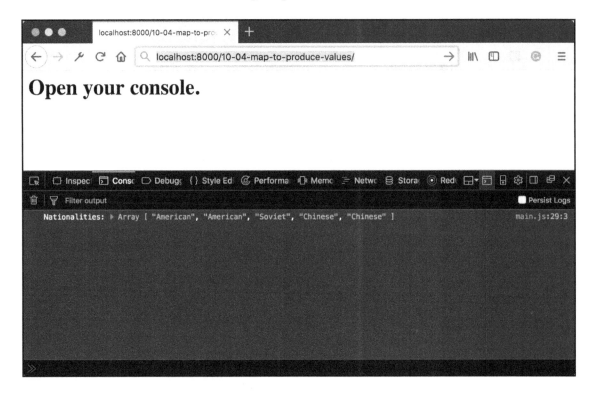

How it works...

The map works similarly to several of the other methods we've seen so far. It takes a function that receives an array element as a parameter and returns some value. Those values are collected into a new array, and that new array is returned by the map method.

Using Array.reduce to transform data

The map method is great for creating data that maps directly to elements from an existing array. However, sometimes, the desired result takes on a different shape. To do this, we can use the reduce method to accumulate values into a new form.

In this recipe, we'll take a look at how to use the reduce method to transform data.

Getting ready

This recipe assumes that you already have a workspace that allows you to create and run ES modules in your browser. If you don't, refer to the first two chapters.

How to do it...

1. Open your command-line application, and navigate to your workspace.
2. Create a new folder named `10-05-reduce-to-transform-data`.
3. Create a `main.js` file that defines a new `class` named `Rocket` that takes a constructor argument `name` and assigns it to an instance property:

```
// main.js
class Rocket {
  constructor(name) {
    this.name = name;
  }
  }
```

4. Create a `main` function with an array of nationality strings:

```
// main.js
export function main() {
  const nationalities = [
    'American',
    'American',
    'Chinese',
    'American',
    'Chinese',
    'Chinese',
    'Soviet',
    'Soviet'
  ];
}
```

5. Use the `reduce` method to count the different nationalities:

```
// main.js
export function main() {
  //...
  const nationalityCount = nationalities.reduce((acc,
  nationality) => {
    acc[nationality] = acc[nationality] || 0;
    acc[nationality] ++;
```

```
        return acc;
      }, {});

      console.log('Nationalities:', nationalityCount);
    }
```

6. Start your Python web server and open the following link in your browser: `http://localhost:8000/`.

7. You should see the following output:

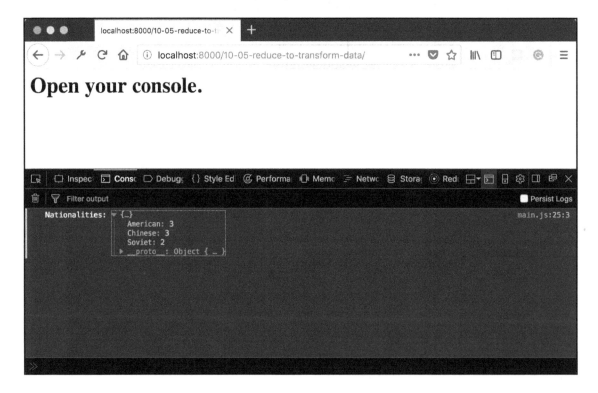

How it works...

Like other methods we've seen previously, the `reduce` method visits each element in an array. However, it takes a different set of parameters. The first parameter is a function that receives two arguments, an accumulator and the current element. The result of this function is the new accumulated value.

The second argument is the initial value of the accumulator.

In the recipe, the accumulator is initialized as an empty object. The function then uses the current array value as a key and increments a counter for that key. In this way, we count the number of times each key appears.

We can see that, unlike with `map`, the resulting data shape is different from the initial array.

Extracting array members with destructuring

Indexing arrays directly is relatively simple. The syntax is familiar to all but the most novice developers. However, what is also familiar is *off by one error*. This means that an array or a collection has been indexed incorrectly by a single position. In some cases, this will cause a fault that is immediately recognizable. Other times, it will cause more subtle errors.

In this recipe, we'll take a look at how to extract members of an array with destructuring syntax.

Getting ready

This recipe assumes that you already have a workspace that allows you to create and run ES modules in your browser. If you don't, refer to the first two chapters.

How to do it...

1. Open your command-line application, and navigate to your workspace.
2. Create a new folder named `10-06-extract-array-members-with-destructuring`.

3. Create a `main.js` file that defines a new `class` named `Rocket` that takes a constructor argument `name` and assigns it to an instance property:

```
// main.js
class Rocket {
  constructor(name) {
    this.name = name;
  }
}
```

4. Create a `main` function with an array of rockets:

```
// main.js
export function main() {
  const rockets = [
    new Rocket('US: Saturn V'),
    new Rocket('US: Falcon Heavy'),
    new Rocket('USSR: Soyuz'),
    new Rocket('CN: Dong Feng'),
    new Rocket('CN: Long March')
  ]
}
```

5. Use the destructuring syntax to assign each member to a local variable:

```
// main.js
export function main() {
  //...
  const [
    saturnV,
    falconHeavy,
    soyuz,
    dongFeng,
    longMarch
  ] = rockets;

  console.log(saturnV, falconHeavy, soyuz, dongFeng,
longMarch);
}
```

6. Start your Python web server and open the following link in your browser: `http://localhost:8000/`.

7. You should see the following output:

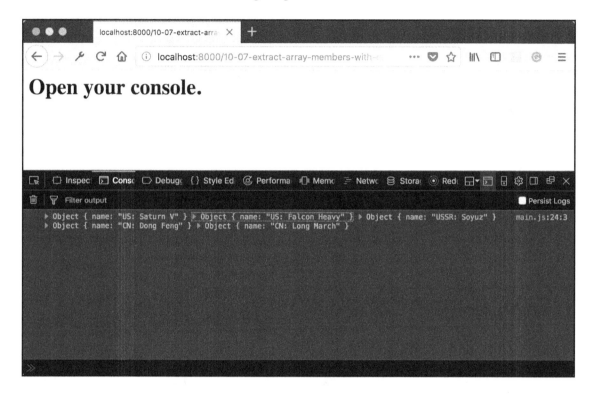

How it works...

The above recipe shows how to use destructuring syntax to create individual variables for elements in an array. The destructuring syntax mirrors the indices of the corresponding array. So, variable names will be associated with the element at the corresponding position in the array. The name at the zero[th] position will be assigned a value at the beginning of the array. The name at position 1 will be assigned the value at the next, and so on.

So we can see above that we name each of the elements in the `rockets` array. The value of each of the extracted elements is a match for the corresponding rocket.

Getting the head and tail of array using the rest operator

Using destructuring to pick out elements is convenient, but we don't always want to pull out every element. A commonly useful pattern is to get the zeroth element of an array assigned to one variable, and the rest of the elements in another. This is commonly called the head and tail of an array.

In this recipe, we'll take a look at how to use the rest operator to get the head and tail of an array.

Getting ready

This recipe assumes that you already have a workspace that allows you to create and run ES modules in your browser. If you don't, refer to the first two chapters.

How to do it...

1. Open your command-line application, and navigate to your workspace.
2. Create a new folder named `10-07-get-head-and-tail-from-array`.
3. Create a `main.js` file that defines a new `class` named `Rocket` that takes a constructor argument `name` and assigns it to an instance property:

```
// main.js
class Rocket {
  constructor(name) {
    this.name = name;
  }
}
```

4. Create a `main` function with an array of rockets:

```
// main.js
export function main() {
  const rockets = [
    new Rocket('US: Saturn V'),
    new Rocket('US: Falcon Heavy'),
    new Rocket('USSR: Soyuz'),
    new Rocket('CN: Dong Feng'),
    new Rocket('CN: Long March')
```

```
            ]
        }
```

5. Use the destructuring syntax and the rest operator to get the head and the tail of the array:

```
// main.js
export function main() {
    //...
    const [saturnV, ...otherRockets] = rockets;
    console.log(saturnV);
    console.log(otherRockets)
}
```

6. Start your Python web server and open the following link in your browser: `http://localhost:8000/`.

7. You should see the following output:

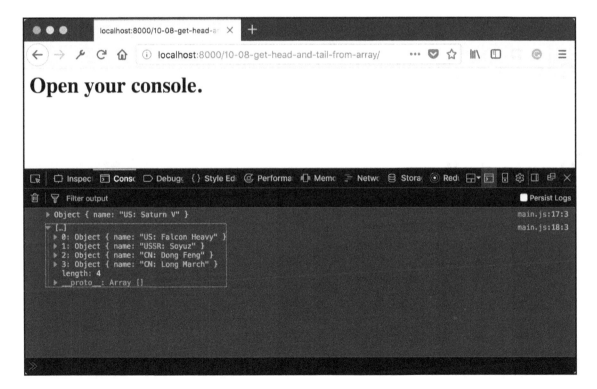

How it works...

The first element `saturnV` works in the same manner as the preceding recipe. The rest operator indicates that the remaining elements should be assigned to the `otherRockets` variable. Since it isn't necessarily a single element, this will be an array.

It should be noted that the rest operator must be the last member of the destructuring syntax. If it is followed by a comma, you will receive a parse error.

Combining arrays with the spread operator

We have seen how to use some new syntax to extract elements from an array. Not to be left out, there are also some new facilities for combining arrays. Helpfully, as we'll see, the use of the spread operator mirrors that of the rest operator.

In this recipe, we'll take a look at how to use the spread operator to combine arrays.

Getting ready

This recipe assumes that you already have a workspace that allows you to create and run ES modules in your browser. If you don't, refer to the first two chapters.

How to do it...

1. Open your command-line application, and navigate to your workspace.
2. Create a new folder named `10-08-combine-arrays-using-spread`.
3. Create a `main.js` file that defines a new `class` named `Rocket` that takes a constructor argument `name` and assigns it to an instance property:

```
// main.js
class Rocket {
  constructor(name) {
    this.name = name;
  }
  }
```

4. Create a `main` function with multiple array rockets, divided by nationality, and a standalone `Rocket` variable:

```
// main.js
export function main() {
  const usRockets= [
    new Rocket('US: Saturn V'),
    new Rocket('US: Falcon Heavy')
  ];

  const sovietRocket = new Rocket('USSR: Soyuz');

  const chineseRockets = [
    new Rocket('CN: Dong Feng'),
    new Rocket('CN: Long March')
  ];
}
```

5. Use the structuring syntax and the spread operator to combine the rockets into a single array:

```
// main.js
export function main() {
  //...
  const rockets = [...usRockets, sovietRocket,
  ...chineseRockets];
  console.log(rockets);
}
```

6. Start your Python web server and open the following link in your browser: `http://localhost:8000/`.

7. You should see the following output:

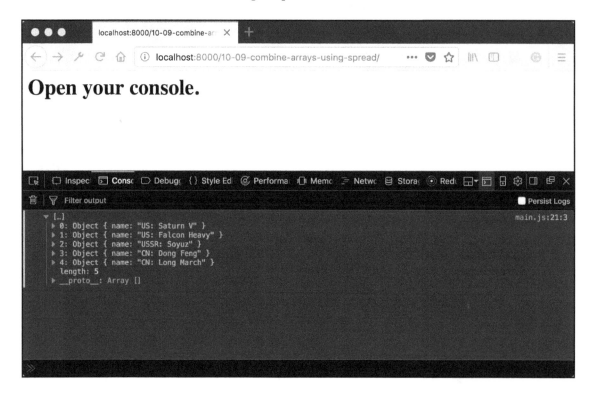

How it works...

The way I think about the rest operator is to think of it *spreading* members of the collection out into the current collection. In the preceding recipe, this means that the members of usRockets and chineseRockets are spread out into the new array, rockets.

This spreading means that they can be referenced in the same syntactic level as the standalone sovietRocket when creating the new array. This combining of elements into a new structure is sometimes referred to as *structuring*, mirroring the *destructuring* terminology.

11
Working with Maps and Symbols

In this chapter, we will cover the following recipes:

- Using Symbol to create a local instance
- Using Symbol.for to create a global instance
- Using Symbol to simulate enums
- Setting and deleting entries from Map
- Creating a Map from the existing data
- Creating a class that wraps Map to work with specific complex types
- Setting and deleting entries from WeakMap
- Creating a WeakMap from existing data
- Creating a class that uses WeakMap to work with specific complex types

Introduction

We saw how to use ECMAScript classical semantics to concisely express more sophisticated relationships between data and operations. We also saw how to take advantage of expanded APIs for existing types (object and array). However, ECMAScript has more to offer. Among the new types are Symbol, Map, and cousin of Map, that is, WeakMap. These types, to some extent, could be simulated in earlier versions of JavaScript, but now are readily available and have native support.

The recipes in this chapter will illustrate some uses of these types, both together and in isolation.

Using Symbol to create a local instance

Symbols on their own aren't particularly useful, but they are very useful as keys for other data structures. They are well suited as keys because it is possible to restrict the access to their values. There are two ways these comparisons can work. We can create local symbols, which are unique and can be recreated after initialization, and global symbols, which can be referenced by their constructor value.

In this recipe, we'll take a look at how to use Symbol as a function to create local symbols. This means that each instance will be new, even if the same arguments are used.

Getting ready

This recipe assumes that you already have a workspace that allows you to create and run ES modules in your browser. If you don't, refer to the first two chapters.

How to do it...

1. Open your command-line application and navigate to your workspace.
2. Create a new folder named 11-01-local-symbols.
3. Copy or create an index.html that loads and runs a main function from main.js.

4. Create a `main.js` file that defines a `main` function that creates a couple of sets of symbols using the same arguments. Print out their equality as follows:

```
// main.js
export function main() {
    const usLaunchLocation = Symbol.for('Kennedy Space
Center');
    const duplicateLaunchLocation = Symbol.for('Kennedy Space
    Center');
    console.log(usLaunchLocation, duplicateLaunchLocation);
    console.log('Identical launch locations: ',
usLaunchLocation
    === duplicateLaunchLocation);
    const rocketNumber = Symbol.for(5);
    const duplicateRocketNumber = Symbol.for(5);
    const stringDuplicateRocketNumber = Symbol.for("5");
    console.log(rocketNumber, duplicateRocketNumber,
    stringDuplicateRocketNumber);
    console.log('Identical rocket numbers: ', rocketNumber ===
    duplicateRocketNumber);
    console.log(
        'Identical string rocket numbers: ',
        rocketNumber ===    stringDuplicateRocketNumber
    );
}
```

5. Use `Symbol.keyFor` to note the `key` for the rocket number `Symbol`:

```
// main.js
export function main() {
    // ...
    console.log(Symbol.keyFor(rocketNumber),
    Symbol.keyFor(stringDuplicateRocketNumber));
    // print type
    console.log(
        typeof Symbol.keyFor(rocketNumber),
        typeof Symbol.keyFor(stringDuplicateRocketNumber)
    )
}
```

6. Start your Python web server and open the following link in your browser: `http://localhost:8000/`.

7. You should see the following output:

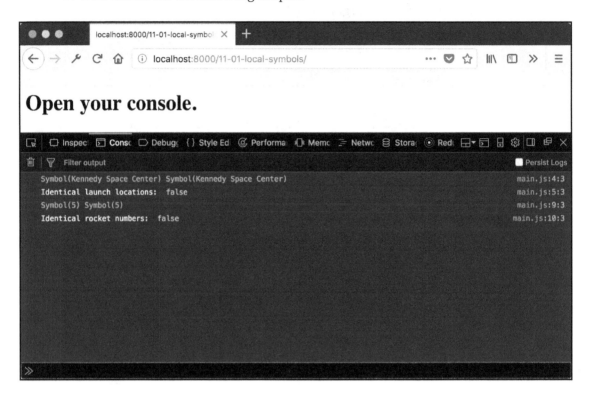

How it works...

When creating a `Symbol` with the `Symbol.for` method, the instance returned may be a preexisting instance. We can see this when we create a `Symbol` with the same string and number values. We can even see the same instance when a number is provided as a string.

When printing out the types for the keys, we can see why the numbers match, even when the argument is a string. When we retrieve a key for a numeric value, it is converted to a string, and thus is equivalent to the string representation of the number.

Using Symbol.for to create a global instance

We've seen how to create unique symbols to use as keys in a local context. However, sometimes, we want to be able to interact with a data structure. Symbols can be made to work in this case as well.

Getting ready

This recipe assumes that you already have a workspace that allows you to create and run ES modules in your browser. If you don't, refer to the first two chapters.

How to do it...

1. Open your command-line application and navigate to your workspace.
2. Create a new folder named `11-02-symbol-for-global`.
3. Copy or create an `index.html` that loads and runs a `main` function from `main.js`.
4. Create a `main.js` file that defines a `main` function that creates a couple of sets of Symbols, using `Symbol.for`, with string and number arguments. Compare the numeric symbols with a number as string:

```
// main.js
export function main() {
  const usLaunchLocation = Symbol.for('Kennedy Space Center');
  const duplicateLaunchLocation = Symbol.for('Kennedy Space
  Center');
  console.log(usLaunchLocation, duplicateLaunchLocation);
  console.log('Identical launch locations: ', usLaunchLocation
  === duplicateLaunchLocation);

  const rocketNumber = Symbol.for(5);
  const duplicateRocketNumber = Symbol.for(5);
  const badDuplicateRocketNumber = Symbol.for('5');
  console.log(rocketNumber, duplicateRocketNumber,
  badDuplicateRocketNumber);
  console.log('Identical rocket numbers: ', rocketNumber ===
  duplicateRocketNumber);
  console.log('Identical bad rocket numbers: ', rocketNumber
  === duplicateRocketNumber);
}
```

5. Start your Python web server and open the following link in your browser: `http://localhost:8000/`.

6. You should see the following output:

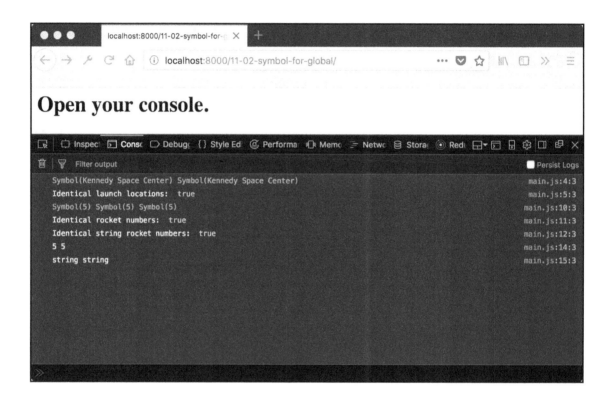

How it works...

The `slice` method takes two parameters, a start index and an end index. The end index is noninclusive. This means that the new set will include the elements between the start and end index, including the element at the start index, but not the element at the end index.

This might seem a bit confusing, but think of it this way, consider that the start index is two and the end index is three. The difference between those two numbers is one, and there is a single element in the resulting subset. For indices *0* and *2*, the difference is two and there will be two elements in the resulting subset.

Using Symbol to simulate enums

We've seen how to create `Symbol` that can be accessed globally, and those that can't be accessed outside of their initial context. Now, we'll see how to use them to create something that wasn't really possible in earlier versions of JavaScript.

In this recipe, we'll use local `Symbol` to simulate a type that is available in many other languages, enums.

Getting ready

This recipe assumes that you already have a workspace that allows you to create and run ES modules in your browser. If you don't, refer to the first two chapters.

How to do it...

1. Open your command-line application and navigate to your workspace.
2. Create a new folder named `11-03-symbols-simulate-enums`.
3. Create a `main.js` file that defines a new `object` named `LaunchSite`, property values of the object should be local `Symbols`:

```
// main.js
const LaunchSite = {
  KENNEDY_SPACE_CENTER: Symbol('Kennedy Space Center'),
  WHITE_SANDS: Symbol('White Sands Missile Range'),
  BAIKONUR: Symbol('Baikonur Cosmodrome'),
  BROGLIO: Symbol('Broglio Space Center'),
  VIKRAM_SARABHAI: Symbol('Vikram Sarabhai Space Centre')
}
```

4. Create a `main` function and compare the value of an enum entry to different values:

```
// main.js
export function main() {
  console.log("Kennedy Space Center Site: ",
LaunchSite.KENNEDY_SPACE_CENTER);
  console.log("Duplicate String: ",
LaunchSite.KENNEDY_SPACE_CENTER === 'Kennedy Space Center');
  console.log("Duplicate Symbol: ",
LaunchSite.KENNEDY_SPACE_CENTER === Symbol('Kennedy Space
```

```
Center'));
  console.log("Duplicate Global Symbol: ",
LaunchSite.KENNEDY_SPACE_CENTER === Symbol.for('kennedy Space
Center'));
}
```

5. Start your Python web server and open the following link in your browser:
   `http://localhost:8000/`.

6. You should see the following output:

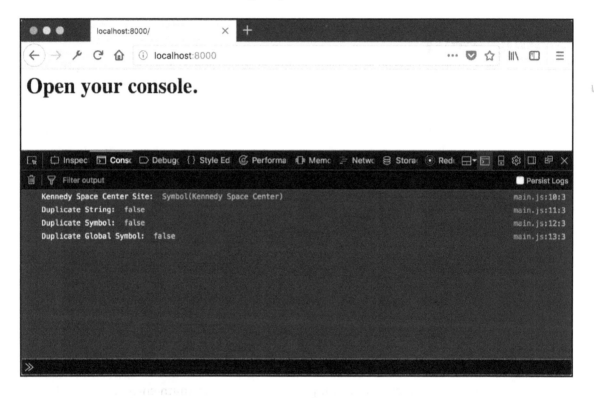

How it works...

As mentioned before, the local `Symbol` instances will be unique every time they are created. Thus, we aren't able to recreate the `Symbol` value in the `main` function. This means that any code expecting a value from that enum can't be coerced with an equivalent value.

One use in which enum types are valuable is as options. Imagine an options object, one of the options needs to be able to take multiple values (say animation tweening). A string value would get the job done but can easily be miss-typed. With an enum, the user of a function must reference that enum; this is less brittle and clearer when reading afterward.

Setting and deleting entries from Map

The rest of this chapter will focus on new data structures added in ECMAScript. To some extent, they can be simulated in ES5. However, native support and explicit naming make code that utilizes these features more efficient and clearer.

In this recipe, we'll take a look at the basics of adding and removing entries from a Map using the set and delete methods.

Getting ready

This recipe assumes that you already have a workspace that allows you to create and run ES modules in your browser. If you don't, refer to the first two chapters.

How to do it...

1. Open your command-line application and navigate to your workspace.
2. Create a new folder named 11-04-set-and-delete-from-map.
3. Create a main.js file that defines a new class named Rocket that takes a constructor argument name and assigns it to an instance property:

```
// main.js
class Rocket {
  constructor(name) {
    this.name = name;
  }
  }
```

4. Create an enum of different launch sites:

```
// main.js
const LaunchSite = {
  KENNEDY_SPACE_CENTER: Symbol('Kennedy Space Center'),
  JUIQUAN: Symbol('Jiuquan Satellite Launch Center'),
  WHITE_SANDS: Symbol('Jiuquan Satellite Launch Center'),
  BAIKONUR: Symbol('Baikonur Cosmodrome')
}
```

5. Create a `main` function. In that function, use the `set` and `delete` methods to manipulate entries of launch site to rocket:

```
// main.js
export function main() {
  const rocketSiteMap = new Map();

  rocketSiteMap.set(LaunchSite.KENNEDY_SPACE_CENTER, new
Rocket('US:
  Saturn V'));
  const falconHeavy = new Rocket('US: Falcon Heavy');
  rocketSiteMap.set(LaunchSite.WHITE_SANDS, falconHeavy);
  console.log(rocketSiteMap.get(LaunchSite.KENNEDY_SPACE_CENTER));
  console.log(rocketSiteMap.get(LaunchSite.WHITE_SANDS));
  rocketSiteMap.set(LaunchSite.KENNEDY_SPACE_CENTER, new
Rocket('US:
  Space Shuttle'));
  rocketSiteMap.delete(LaunchSite.WHITE_SANDS);
  console.log(rocketSiteMap.get(LaunchSite.KENNEDY_SPACE_CENTER));
  console.log(rocketSiteMap.get(LaunchSite.WHITE_SANDS)); }
```

6. Start your Python web server and open the following link in your browser: `http://localhost:8000/`.

7. You should see the following output:

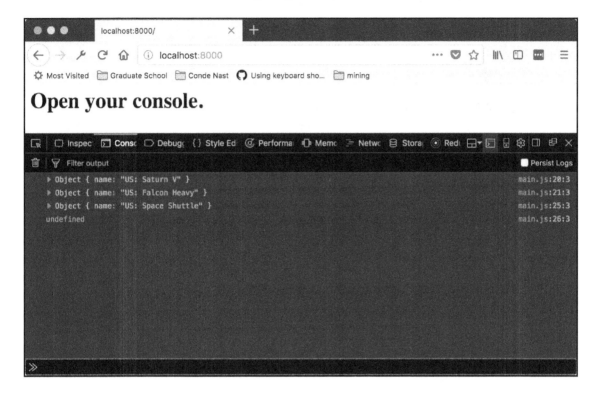

How it works...

The map is a pairing between a `key` and `value`. The keys reference the values when calling the instance of `Map` methods. This pairing is one-to-one; this means that there can only be one value per key. Thus, when we set another rocket to the `KENNEDY_SPACE_CENTER` key, the old value is replaced.

The `delete` method removes the entry corresponding to the `key`. Thus, after `delete`, that particular entry is undefined.

Creating a Map from the existing data

We just saw how to add values individually to maps. This can be tedious, however. For example, if we are working with a dataset that might be very large or unknown ahead of time, it would be nice to initialize a map with a function call rather than hundreds or thousands.

In this recipe, we'll take a look at how to create a new Map with the preexisting data.

Getting ready

This recipe assumes that you already have a workspace that allows you to create and run ES modules in your browser. If you don't, refer to the first two chapters.

How to do it...

1. Open your command-line application and navigate to your workspace.
2. Create a new folder named `11-05-create-map-from-data`.
3. Create a `main.js` file that defines a new `class` named `Rocket` that takes a constructor argument `name` and assigns it to an instance property:

```
// main.js
class Rocket {
  constructor(name) {
    this.name = name;
  }
    }
```

4. Create an enum of various launch sites:

```
// main.js
const LaunchSite = {
  KENNEDY_SPACE_CENTER: Symbol('Kennedy Space Center'),
  JUIQUAN: Symbol('Jiuquan Satellite Launch Center'),
  WHITE_SANDS: Symbol('Jiuquan Satellite Launch Center'),
  BAIKONUR: Symbol('Baikonur Cosmodrome')
}
```

5. Create a `main` function. In that function, create a map with launch site and rocket key value pairs:

```js
// main.js
export function main() {
  const rocketSites = [
    [ LaunchSite.KENNEDY_SPACE_CENTER, new Rocket('US: Saturn
    V'),],
    [ LaunchSite.WHITE_SANDS, new Rocket('US: Falcon Heavy') ],
    [ LaunchSite.BAIKONUR, new Rocket('USSR: Soyuz') ],
    [ LaunchSite.JUIQUAN, new Rocket('CN: Long March') ] ]

  const rocketSiteMap = new Map(rocketSites);
  console.log(rocketSiteMap)
}
```

6. Start your Python web server and open the following link in your browser: `http://localhost:8000/`.

7. You should see the following output:

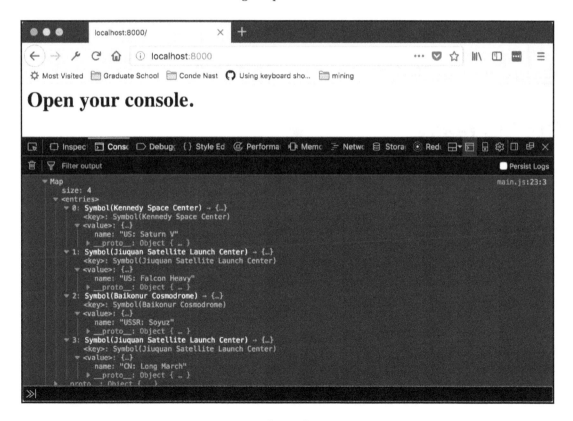

How it works...

As said before, the map is a pairing between a `key` and `value`. The `Map` constructor expects an `iterable` collection of key-value pairs. In the preceding recipe, we've passed a two-dimensional array. The outer dimension is the `iterable` that contains multiple entries.

The inner dimension is the key-value pair. The first member of the key-value is the launch site. The second member is the `value` (in our case, a `Rocket`). The `Map` constructor iterates over the entries provided and creates a pairing between each.

Creating a class that wraps Map to work with specific complex types

When working with a large collection, it can be nice to know what kind of object to expect when picking out on a member. Normally, JavaScript collections are heterogeneous, meaning that any type can be used. In the case of `Map`, this means that either `key` or `value` can take on any type.

In this recipe, we'll take a look at how to create a wrapper class for `Map` in order to control what types are used in the `Map`.

Getting ready

This recipe assumes that you already have a workspace that allows you to create and run ES modules in your browser. If you don't, refer to the first two chapters.

How to do it...

1. Open your command-line application and navigate to your workspace.
2. Create a new folder named `11-06-create-class-to-wrap-map`.

3. Create a `main.js` file that defines a new `class` named `Rocket` that takes a constructor argument `name` and assigns it to an instance property:

```
// main.js
class Rocket {
  constructor(name) {
    this.name = name;
  }
}
```

4. Create a class named `RocketSiteMap` file that creates a new map and assigns it as an instance property in the constructor:

```
// main.js
class RocketSiteMap {
  constructor () {
    this.map = new Map();
  }
}
```

5. Add the `set` method that checks the type of the `key` and `value` arguments. This method should throw an error if the argument types are incorrect, otherwise set the pair as an entry on the map:

```
// main.js
class RocketSiteMap {
  set (site, rocket) {
    if (!(rocket instanceof Rocket)) {
      throw new Error('Value of `RocketMap` must be of type
      `Rocket`');
    }
    else if (typeof site !== 'symbol') {
      throw new Error('Key of `RocketMap` must be of type
      `Symbol`');
    }
    this.map.set(site, rocket);
  }
}
```

6. Add a `get` method that returns the entry for `key` from the map:

```
// main.js
class RocketSiteMap {
  get (key) {
    return this.get(key);
  }
```

7. Create an enum of various launch sites:

```
// main.js
const LaunchSite = {
  KENNEDY_SPACE_CENTER: Symbol('Kennedy Space Center'),
  JUIQUAN: Symbol('Jiuquan Satellite Launch Center'),
  WHITE_SANDS: Symbol('Jiuquan Satellite Launch Center'),
  BAIKONUR: Symbol('Baikonur Cosmodrome')
}
```

8. Create a `main` function. Attempt to set various `key` and `value` pairs to an instance of `RocketMap`:

```
// main.js
export function main() {
  const rocketSiteMap = new RocketSiteMap();
  rocketSiteMap.set(LaunchSite.KENNEDY_SPACE_CENTER, new Rocket('US:
  Saturn V'));
  rocketSiteMap.set(LaunchSite.WHITE_SANDS, new Rocket('US:
Falcon
  Heavy'));
  console.log(rocketSiteMap)

  try {
    rocketSiteMap.set(LaunchSite.KENNEDY_SPACE_CENTER, 'Buzz
    Lightyear');
  } catch (e) {
    console.error(e);
  }

  try {
    rocketSiteMap.set('Invalid Lanch Site', new Rocket('Long
    March'));
  } catch (e) {
    console.error(e);
  }
}
```

9. Start your Python web server and open the following link in your browser: `http://localhost:8000/`.

10. You should see the following output:

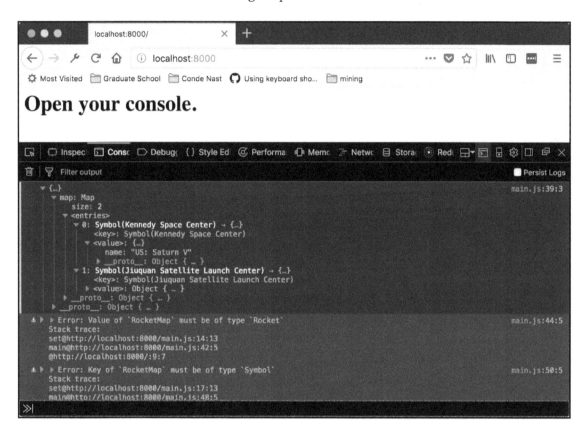

How it works...

From the implementation of the `set` method, we can see where the types of the arguments are being checked. `Symbol`, as a type, doesn't have a constructor, so we can't use the `instanceof` operator, but the `typeof` operator returns a `symbol` string we can check against. The `Rocket` instances behave like other instances we've seen in other recipes, and can be checked like the others.

When the incorrect type is passed as an argument to `set`, one of the conditionals will trigger and an error will be thrown.

Setting and deleting entries from WeakMap

We've seen how to use Maps in a variety of situations. There is another new class in ECMAScript that behaves in a very similar way, but has some helpful properties. The `WeakMap`, like `Map`, is a key-value data structure.

In this recipe, we'll take a look at how to add and remove elements from a `WeakMap` with the `set` and `delete` methods. And we'll also see how they differ from the `Map` class.

Getting ready

This recipe assumes that you already have a workspace that allows you to create and run ES modules in your browser. If you don't, refer to the first two chapters.

How to do it...

1. Open your command-line application and navigate to your workspace.
2. Create a new folder named `11-07-set-and-delete-from-weakmap`.
3. Create a `main.js` file that defines a new `class` named `Rocket` that takes a constructor argument `name` and assigns it to an instance property:

```
// main.js
class Rocket {
  constructor(name) {
    this.name = name;
  }
}
```

4. Create an `enum` of various launch sites:

```
// main.js
const LaunchSite = {
  KENNEDY_SPACE_CENTER: Symbol('Kennedy Space Center'),
  JUIQUAN: Symbol('Jiuquan Satellite Launch Center'),
  WHITE_SANDS: Symbol('Jiuquan Satellite Launch Center'),
  BAIKONUR: Symbol('Baikonur Cosmodrome')
}
```

5. Create a `main` function. In that function, use the `set` and `delete` methods to manipulate entries of launch site to rocket. Try to use a `Symbol` as a key:

```
// main.js
export function main() {
  const falconHeavy = new Rocket('US: Falcon Heavy');
  const rocketSiteMap = new WeakMap();

  rocketSiteMap.set(new Rocket('US: Saturn V'),
  LaunchSite.KENNEDY_SPACE_CENTER);
  rocketSiteMap.set(falconHeavy,
  LaunchSite.KENNEDY_SPACE_CENTER);
  console.log(rocketSiteMap)

  rocketSiteMap.delete(falconHeavy);
  console.log(rocketSiteMap)

  // try to set with a symbol; expect error
  rocketSiteMap.set(LaunchSite.KENNEDY_SPACE_CENTER,
  falconHeavy);
}
```

6. Start your Python web server and open the following link in your browser: `http://localhost:8000/`.

7. You should see the following output:

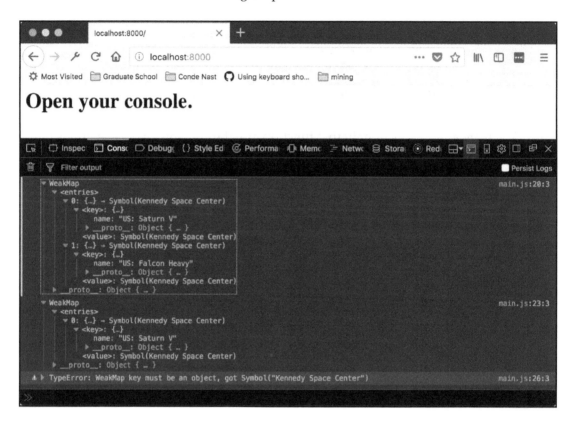

How it works...

Like instances of `Map`, the `WeakMap` instance is a pairing between a `key` and `value`. However, crucially, they differ in what types can be used as keys. `Map` can use any type for keys. `WeakMap` can only have values of the `Object` type as keys. This helps `WeakMap` to be more efficient.

The reason that `WeakMap` can be more efficient has to do with memory management and garbage collection. Consider that Map entries have to be kept around for the lifetime of the program. Since they can use primitive types as keys (Booleans, strings, numbers, and Symbols), these values could be recreated, and those Map entries can be referenced at any time.

WeakMap keys, by contrast, can only be of the Object type. The Object values cannot be recreated; objects with the same values are still different instances. This means that an entry to a WeakMap can only be accessed as long as a reference to the key is available; once that reference is lost, the entry can no longer be accessed.

The entries are no long accessible because the key value doesn't have any existing references to them. This means that the entry can be released from memory (no sense in keeping unused values around). This allows the garbage collector to free up that memory.

 Refer to the Mozilla documentation for more information on WeakMap: https://developer.mozilla.org/en-US/docs/Web/JavaScript/ Reference/Global_Objects/WeakMap.

Creating a WeakMap from existing data

We just saw how to add values individually to a WeakMap and why it is different from a Map. However, it can be tedious to create a WeakMap one entry at a time.

In this recipe, we'll take a look at how to create a new Map with the preexisting data.

Getting ready

This recipe assumes that you already have a workspace that allows you to create and run ES modules in your browser. If you don't, refer to the first two chapters.

If you are unfamiliar with the WeakMap class, refer to the *Setting and deleting entries from WeakMap* recipe.

How to do it...

1. Open your command-line application and navigate to your workspace.
2. Create a new folder named 11-08-create-weakmap-from-data.

3. Create a `main.js` file that defines a new class named `Rocket` that takes a constructor argument `name` and assigns it to an instance property:

```
// main.js
class Rocket {
  constructor(name) {
    this.name = name;
  }
 }
```

4. Create an enum of various launch sites:

```
// main.js
const LaunchSite = {
  KENNEDY_SPACE_CENTER: Symbol('Kennedy Space Center'),
  JUIQUAN: Symbol('Jiuquan Satellite Launch Center'),
  WHITE_SANDS: Symbol('Jiuquan Satellite Launch Center'),
  BAIKONUR: Symbol('Baikonur Cosmodrome')
}
```

5. Create a `main` function. In that function, create a map with launch site and rocket key value pairs:

```
// main.js
export function main() {
  const rocketSites = [
    [ new Rocket('US: Saturn V'),
LaunchSite.KENNEDY_SPACE_CENTER
    ],
    [ new Rocket('US: Falcon Heavy'), LaunchSite.WHITE_SANDS ],
    [ new Rocket('USSR: Soyuz'), LaunchSite.BAIKONUR ],
    [ new Rocket('CN: Dong Feng'), LaunchSite.JUIQUAN ],
    [ new Rocket('CN: Long March'), LaunchSite.JUIQUAN ] ];

  const rocketSiteMap = new WeakMap(rocketSites);
  console.log(rocketSiteMap);
}
```

6. Start your Python web server and open the following link in your browser: `http://localhost:8000/`.

7. You should see the following output:

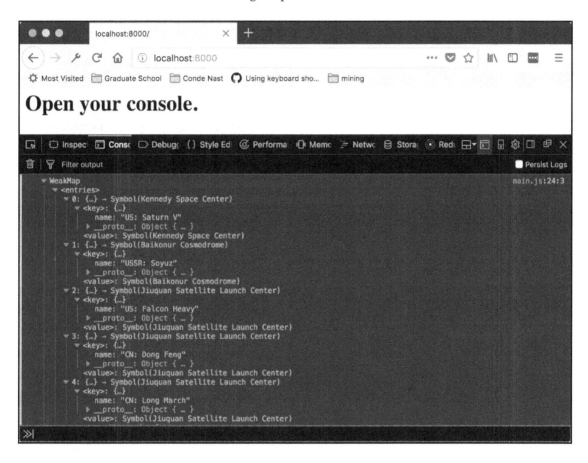

How it works...

No surprises here, the WeakMap constructor adheres to the same interface as Map. The only difference is the type restriction on key. The argument for the constructor is a two-dimensional array, where the outer dimension is the list of entries. The inner dimension represents the key-value pairs. The first member of the inner dimension is the key, and the second is the value.

Creating a class that uses WeakMap to work with specific complex types

Just as with Map, knowing what type to expect from the WeakMap collection can be valuable. The key types are very slightly restricted, but still pretty loose, and there is no restriction on what type the values can be.

In this recipe, we'll take a look at how to create a wrapper class for WeakMap in order to control what types are used in the WeakMap.

Getting ready

This recipe assumes that you already have a workspace that allows you to create and run ES modules in your browser. If you don't, refer to the first two chapters.

If you are unfamiliar with the WeakMap class, refer to the *Setting and deleting entries from WeakMap* recipe.

How to do it...

1. Open your command-line application and navigate to your workspace.
2. Create a new folder named `11-09-create-class-to-wrap-weakmap`.
3. Create a `main.js` file that defines a new class named Rocket that takes a constructor argument name and assigns it to an instance property:

```
// main.js
class Rocket {
  constructor(name) {
    this.name = name;
  }
}
```

4. Create a class named `RocketSiteMap` file that creates a new map and assigns it as an instance property in the constructor:

```
// main.js
class RocketSiteMap {
  constructor () {
    this.map = new WeakMap();
    }
  }
```

5. Add the `set` method that checks the type of the `key` and `value` arguments. This method should throw if the argument types are incorrect, otherwise set the pair as an entry on the map:

```
// main.js
class RocketSiteMap {
set (rocket, site) {
    if (!(rocket instanceof Rocket)) {
      throw new Error('Key of `RocketMap` must be of type
      `Rocket`');
    }
    else if (typeof site !== 'symbol') {
      throw new Error('Values of `RocketMap` must be of type
      `Symbol`');
    }
    this.map.set(rocket, site);
  }

  get (key) {
    return this.get(key);
    }
  }
```

6. Add a `get` method that returns the entry for `key` from the map:

```
// main.js
class RocketSiteMap {
  get (key) {
    return this.get(key);
    }
```

7. Create an enum of various launch sites:

```
// main.js
const LaunchSite = {
  KENNEDY_SPACE_CENTER: Symbol('Kennedy Space Center'),
  JUIQUAN: Symbol('Jiuquan Satellite Launch Center'),
  WHITE_SANDS: Symbol('Jiuquan Satellite Launch Center'),
  BAIKONUR: Symbol('Baikonur Cosmodrome')
}
```

8. Create a `main` function. Attempt to set various `key` and `value` pairs to an instance of `RocketMap`:

```
// main.js
export function main() {
  const rocketSiteMap = new RocketSiteMap();
  rocketSiteMap.set(LaunchSite.KENNEDY_SPACE_CENTER, new
  Rocket('US:
  Saturn V'));
  rocketSiteMap.set(LaunchSite.WHITE_SANDS, new Rocket('US:
  Falcon
  Heavy'));
  console.log(rocketSiteMap)

  try {
    rocketSiteMap.set(LaunchSite.KENNEDY_SPACE_CENTER, 'Buzz
    Lightyear');
  } catch (e) {
    console.error(e);
  }

  try {
    rocketSiteMap.set('Invalid Lanch Site', new Rocket('Long
    March'));
  } catch (e) {
    console.error(e);
  }
}
```

9. Start your Python web server and open the following link in your browser: `http://localhost:8000/`.

10. You should see the following output:

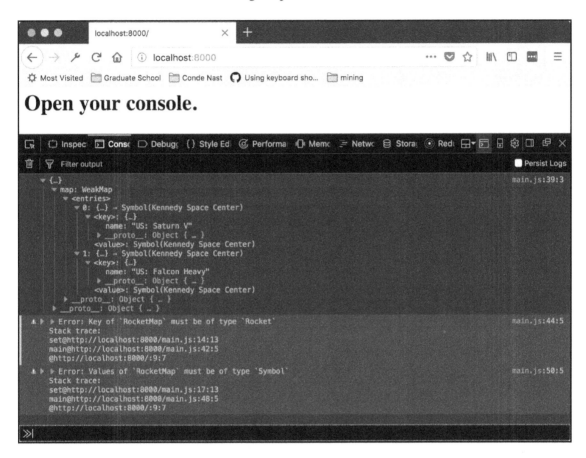

How it works...

From the implementation of the `set` method, we can see where types of the arguments are being checked. `Symbol`, as a type, doesn't have a constructor, so we can't use the `instanceof` operator, but the `typeof` operator returns a symbol string we can check against. The `Rocket` instances behave like other instances we've seen in other recipes, and can be checked like the others.

When the incorrect type is passed as an argument to `set`, one of the conditionals will trigger, and an error will be thrown.

12
Working with Sets

In this chapter, we will cover the following recipes:

- Adding and deleting items from a Set
- Creating a Set from existing data
- Adding and deleting items from a WeakSet
- Creating a WeakSet from existing data
- Finding the union of two sets
- Finding the intersection of two sets
- Finding the difference between two sets
- Creating a class that wraps a Set to work with more complex types

Introduction

For our final chapter, we'll be taking a look at two more new, related types. Set and WeakSet, like Map and WeakMap, are collections of other values. However, rather than creating relationships between pairs of values, Set and WeakSet create a relationship between all entries in the collection. These data structures ensure that there are no duplicated entries. If a new item evaluates as equal with another member, it won't be added to the Set.

The recipes in this chapter will illustrate how to implement different behaviors with the set classes.

Adding and deleting items from a Set

We will start out with the simplest possible tasks involving a Set. In this recipe, we'll take a look at how to add and delete items from a Set using the respective instance methods.

Getting ready

This recipe assumes that you already have a workspace that allows you to create and run ES modules in your browser. If you don't, refer to the first two chapters.

How to do it...

1. Open your command-line application, and navigate to your workspace.
2. Create a new folder named `12-01-add-remove-from-set`.
3. Copy or create an `index.html` that loads and runs a `main` function from `main.js`.
4. Create a `main.js` file that defines a `main` function. In that function, create a new Set instance, then add and remove a few items from it:

```
// main.js
export function main() {
    const rocketSet = new Set();
    rocketSet.add('US: Saturn V');
    rocketSet.add('US: Saturn V');
    rocketSet.add('US: Falcon Heavy');
    console.log(rocketSet);
    rocketSet.delete('US: Falcon Heavy');
    console.log(rocketSet);
}
```

5. Start your Python web server, and open the following URL in your browser: `http://localhost:8000/`.

6. You will see the following output:

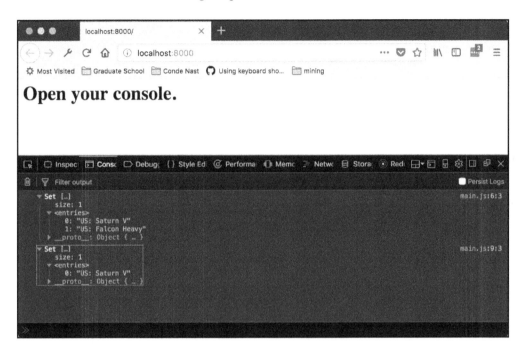

How it works...

A set is a collection of data. But it behaves differently than the more familiar `Array` type. Like mathematical sets, a `Set` instance is meant to only have a single copy of an element. That is, if you had an `Array` of numbers and a `Set` of numbers, the `Array` could contain the number `138` several times, but the `Set` could only contain a single copy if it.

Membership to a Set is evaluated similarly to the `===` operator. In our case, you can see that `US: Saturn V` is only added to the set a single time, despite being provided as an argument to `add` twice. Next, you can see that `US: Falcon Heavy` is removed after being initially added. Subsequently, the set only has a single member.

> To learn more about sets, visit the Mozilla developer documentation at the following link:
> https://developer.mozilla.org/en-US/docs/Web/JavaScript/
> Reference/Global_Objects/Set.

Creating a Set from existing data

We just saw how to add values individually to sets. This can be tedious, however. For example, if we are working with a dataset that might be very large or unknown ahead of time, it would be nice to initialize a map with a function call, rather than hundreds or thousands.

In this recipe, we'll take a look at how to create a new Set with the preexisting data.

Getting ready

This recipe assumes that you already have a workspace that allows you to create and run ES modules in your browser. If you don't, refer to the first two chapters.

How to do it...

1. Open your command-line application, and navigate to your workspace.
2. Create a new folder named `12-02-create-set-from-data`.
3. Copy or create an `index.html` that loads and runs a `main` function from `main.js`.
4. Create a `main.js` file that defines a `main` function with an array of string. Create a new set with that array as a constructor argument:

```
// main.js
export function main() {
  const rockets = [
    'US: Saturn V',
    'US: Falcon Heavy',
    'USSR: Soyuz',
    'CN: Long March',
    'US: Saturn V',
    'US: Saturn V'
  ];

  const rocketSet = new Set(rockets);
  console.log(rockets);
}
```

5. Start your Python web server, and the following URL in your browser:
`http://localhost:8000/`.

6. You should see the following output:

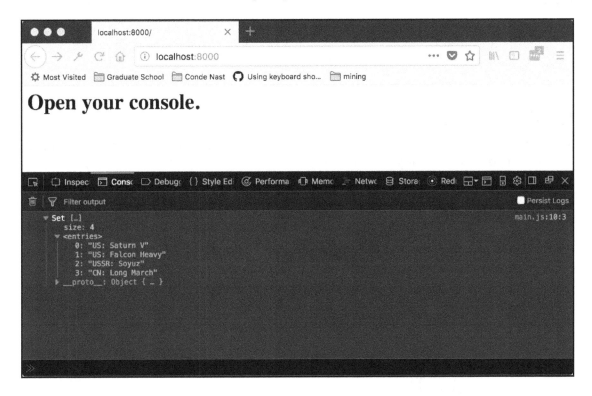

How it works...

In the preceding recipe we see how to create a Set with existing data. The constructor for a Set takes an iterable as an argument. The most familiar iterable is an array. In the case of the Set, each element in the iterable (array) is added to the collection in order. As we mentioned in the preceding recipe, membership of a Set is determined using a similar comparison to the === operator. Sets don't allow duplicate values. Thus, we only see a single US: Saturn V in the <entries> section of the output.

Adding and deleting items from WeakSet

Now, we'll take a look at the corresponding weak data structure, WeakSet. In this recipe, we'll look at how to add and delete items from a WeakSet, using the respective instance methods, and at some restrictions on membership.

Getting ready

This recipe assumes that you already have a workspace that allows you to create and run ES modules in your browser. If you don't, refer to the first two chapters.

How to do it...

1. Open your command-line application, and navigate to your workspace.
2. Create a new folder named 12-03-add-remove-from-weak-set.
3. Copy or create an index.html that loads and runs a main function from main.js.
4. Create a main.js file that defines a new class named Rocket that takes a constructor argument name and assigns it to an instance property:

```
// main.js
class Rocket {
  constructor(name) {
    this.name = name;
  }
}
```

5. Create a main function with some Rocket instances and a WeakMap instance. Add and remove the instances from the set:

```
// main.js
export function main() {
const saturnV = new Rocket('US: Saturn V');
const falconHeavy = new Rocket('US: Falcon Heavy');
const rocketSet = new WeakSet();
rocketSet.add(saturnV);
rocketSet.add(saturnV);
rocketSet.add(falconHeavy);
console.log(rocketSet);
rocketSet.delete(falconHeavy);
console.log(rocketSet);
```

```
// throw error
rocketSet.add('Saturn V');
}
```

6. Start your Python web server, and open the following URL in your browser: `http://localhost:8000/`.

7. You will see the following output:

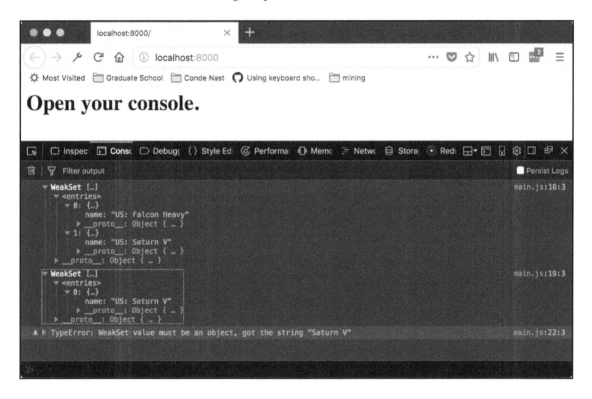

How it works...

Membership to a `WeakSet` is evaluated similarly to the `===` operator. Looking at the preceding, we can see that two `Rocket` instances with the name `US: Saturn V` are added to the set. This is, of course, because the set isn't comparing name properties, but object instances. Thus, we'll see two rather than one (unique names) or three (number of times added) `US: Saturn V` entries.

Next, you can see that the `US: Falcon Heavy` is removed after being initially added. Subsequently, the set doesn't have that member.

An error is thrown when trying to add a string to the `WeakSet`. Like the keys of `WeakMap`, the elements of `WeakSet` must be objects. This is so that the `WeakSet` can only keep weak references to its entries. Thus, the memory allocated for the entries can be released when other references go out of scope.

Creating a WeakSet from existing data

We just saw how to create a Set from existing data. The related class `WeakSet` can be created in a similar way, but has restrictions on membership. In this recipe, we'll take a look at how to create a `WeakSet` from existing data and some restrictions on membership.

Getting ready

This recipe assumes that you already have a workspace that allows you to create and run ES modules in your browser. If you don't, refer to the first two chapters.

How to do it...

1. Open your command-line application, and navigate to your workspace.
2. Create a new folder named `12-04-create-weak-set-from-data`.
3. Create a `main.js` file that defines a new class named `Rocket` that takes a constructor argument `name` and assigns it to an instance property:

```js
// main.js
class Rocket {
  constructor(name) {
    this.name = name;
  }
}
```

4. Create a `main` function with an array of rocket instances. Create a new `WeakSet` from the array. Try to add a string to `WeakSet`:

```js
// main.js
export function main() {
  const rockets = [
    new Rocket('US: Saturn V'),
    new Rocket('US: Saturn V'),
    new Rocket('US: Saturn V'),
    new Rocket('USSR: Soyuz') ,
    new Rocket('CN: Long March')
  ]

  const rocketSet = new WeakSet(rockets);
  console.log(rockets);
}
```

5. Start your Python web server, and open the following URL in your browser: `http://localhost:8000/`.

6. You should see the following output:

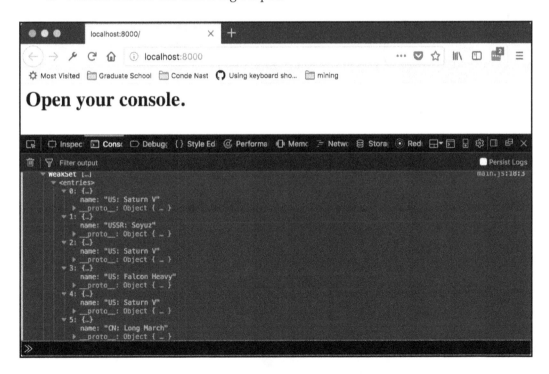

How it works...

Just like the Set constructor, the `WeakSet` constructor takes an iterable. Each element of the array is added in turn. We'll note that multiple instances have the same `name` property. This is, of course, because they are separate `Rocket` instances, despite having the same name value.

Finding the union of two sets

Now that we've got a good handle on sets, it's time to start performing some set operations. Sets are unordered groups of things; something you might want to do is to combine two groups into one. This operation is called a `union` of two sets. An element is in the union of two sets, if it exists in either of them.

In this recipe, we'll take a look at how to create a union of two `Set` instances.

Getting ready

This recipe assumes that you already have a workspace that allows you to create and run ES modules in your browser. If you don't, refer to the first two chapters.

How to do it...

1. Open your command-line application, and navigate to your workspace.
2. Create a new folder named `12-05-set-union`.
3. Create a `main.js` file that defines a new class named `Rocket` that takes a constructor argument `name` and assigns it to an instance property:

```
// main.js
class Rocket {
  constructor(name) {
    this.name = name;
  }
  }
```

4. Create a function called `union` that takes two set arguments:

```
// main.js
function union (set1, set2) {}
```

5. Create a `result` set. Loop through both set instances, and add each `entry` to the resultant set:

```
// main.js
function union (set1, set2) {
  const result = new Set();

  set1.forEach((entry) => result.add(entry));
  set2.forEach((entry) => result.add(entry));

  return result;
}
```

6. Create a `main` function. Create a couple of sets with overlapping members. Log out from the union of the two sets:

```
// main.js
export function main() {
  const usRockets = [
    new Rocket('US: Saturn V'),
    new Rocket('US: Falcon Heavy')
  ];
  const americanSet = new Set(usRockets);
  console.log('American Set', americanSet);

  const allRockets = usRockets.concat([
    new Rocket('USSR: Soyuz'),
    new Rocket('CN: Long March')
  ]);

  const fullSet = new Set(allRockets);
  console.log('Full Set', fullSet);

  console.log('Union', union(americanSet, fullSet));
}
```

7. Start your Python web server, and open the following URL in your browser: `http://localhost:8000/`.

8. You should see the following output:

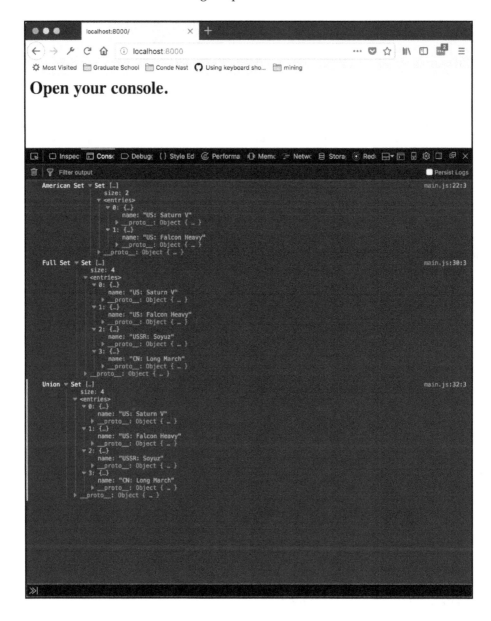

How it works...

In the preceding recipe, we rely on the properties of Set to implement the union operation. As stated before, sets do not store duplicate entries. So, when creating the union, we don't have to worry about adding duplicates to the resulting set, because that is taken care of for us by the class. Simply looping over all the members and adding them is sufficient to create the union set.

Finding the intersection of two sets

Next, we'll take a look at how to find out the elements two Sets have in common. This operation is called an intersection of two sets. An element is in the intersection of two sets, if it exists in both of them.

In this recipe, we'll see how to create an intersection of two Set instances.

Getting ready

This recipe assumes that you already have a workspace that allows you to create and run ES modules in your browser. If you don't, refer to the first two chapters.

How to do it...

1. Open your command-line application, and navigate to your workspace.
2. Create a new folder named 12-06-set-intersection.
3. Create a main.js file that defines a new class named Rocket that takes a constructor argument name and assigns it to an instance property:

```
// main.js
class Rocket {
  constructor(name) {
    this.name = name;
  }
   }
```

4. Create a function called `intersection` that takes two `set` arguments:

```js
// main.js
function intersection (set1, set2) {}
```

5. Create a `result` set. Loop through the first `set` instance. Add each `entry` to the resultant `set`, if it appears in the second `set` as well:

```js
// main.js
function intersection (set1, set2) {
  const result = new Set();

  set1.forEach((entry) => {
    if (set2.has(entry)) {
      result.add(entry);
    }
  });

  return result;
}
```

6. Create a `main` function. Create a couple of sets with overlapping members. Log out the intersection of the two sets:

```js
// main.js
export function main() {
  const usRockets = [
    new Rocket('US: Saturn V'),
    new Rocket('US: Falcon Heavy')
  ];
  const americanSet = new Set(usRockets);
  console.log('American Set', americanSet);

  const allRockets = usRockets.concat([
    new Rocket('USSR: Soyuz'),
    new Rocket('CN: Long March')
  ]);

  const fullSet = new Set(allRockets);
  console.log('Full Set', fullSet);

  console.log('Intersetion', intersection(americanSet,
fullSet));
  }
```

7. Start your Python web server, and open the following URL in your browser: `http://localhost:8000/`.

8. You should see the following output:

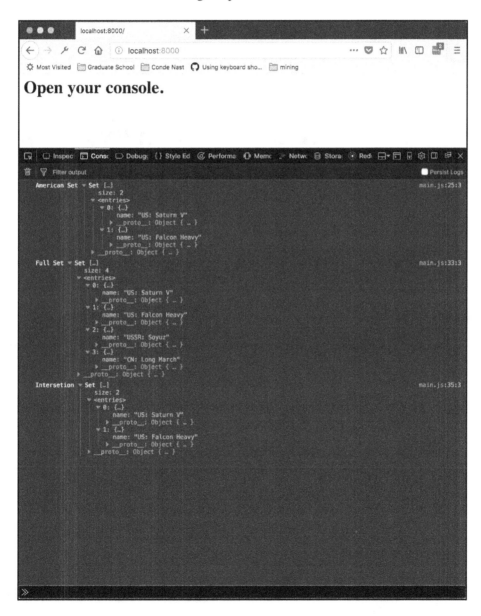

How it works...

An intersection of two sets is defined as all the elements that appear in both sets. In this recipe, we use the has method to implement an intersection operation. We loop over the elements of the first Set and check whether the second contains each element. If the second Set contains that element, then the has method will return true. If this method returns true, then we know that the element is in both Set instances, and we add it to the new intersection.

Finding the difference between two sets

We've seen how to combine two sets with the union operation, and find their common elements with the intersection operation. The logical next step is to see how the sets differ. Next, we'll take a look at how to find out what elements one set has that another doesn't. This operation is called a difference of two sets. An element is in the difference of two sets, if it is in the first set, but not the second.

In this recipe, we'll take a look at how to find the difference between two Set instances.

Getting ready

This recipe assumes that you already have a workspace that allows you to create and run ES modules in your browser. If you don't, refer to the first two chapters.

How to do it...

1. Open your command-line application, and navigate to your workspace.
2. Create a new folder named 12-07-set-difference.
3. Create a main.js file that defines a new class named Rocket that takes a constructor argument name and assigns it to an instance property:

```
// main.js
class Rocket {
  constructor(name) {
    this.name = name;
  }
}
```

4. Create a function called `difference` that takes two `set` arguments:

```
// main.js
function intersection (set1, set2) {}
```

5. Create a `result` set. Loop through the first set instance. Add each entry to the resultant set, if it does not appear in the second `set`:

```
// main.js
function difference(set1, set2) {
  const result = new Set ();

  set1.forEach((entry) => {
    if (!set2.has(entry)) {
      result.add(entry)
    }
  });

  return result;
}
```

6. Create a `main` function. Create a couple of sets with overlapping members. Log out the differences of the two sets:

```
// main.js
export function main() {
  const usRockets = [
    new Rocket('US: Saturn V'),
    new Rocket('US: Falcon Heavy')
  ];
  const americanSet = new Set(usRockets);
  console.log('American Set', americanSet);

  const allRockets = usRockets.concat([
    new Rocket('USSR: Soyuz'),
    new Rocket('CN: Long March')
  ]);

  const fullSet = new Set(allRockets);
  console.log('Full Set', fullSet);

  console.log('Difference 1', difference(americanSet,
fullSet));
  console.log('Difference 2', difference(fullSet,
americanSet));
}
```

7. Start your Python web server, and open the following URL in your browser: `http://localhost:8000/`.

8. You should see the following output:

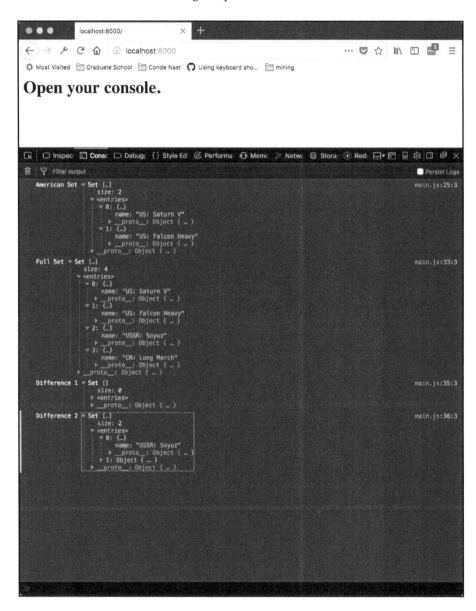

How it works...

In the preceding recipe, we rely on the `has` method on the `Set` class that implements the `difference` operation. An element of a `difference` must appear in the first set but not the second. When looping over the first set, we know that the element is part of the first. Next, we simply have to check whether it is in the second using the `has` method. If this method returns false, then we know that the element is in the difference.

An important distinction between difference and the other two operations we've seen (union and intersection) is that it is not commutative, that is, the order of arguments matters. You can see in the preceding recipe that the result of the difference function changes depending on which set is being differentiated from the other.

Creating a class that wraps a Set to work with more complex types

Knowing what types we are working with is valuable. `WeakSet` has some restriction on membership, but as you may know, objects can vary quite a lot.

In this recipe, we'll take a look at how to create a wrapper class for `Map` in order to control what types are used in the `Map`.

Getting ready

This recipe assumes that you already have a workspace that allows you to create and run ES modules in your browser. If you don't, refer to the first two chapters.

If you are unfamiliar with the `WeakMap` class, refer to the *Setting and deleting entries from a WeakMap* recipe.

How to do it...

1. Open your command-line application, and navigate to your workspace.
2. Create a new folder named `12-08-create-class-to-wrap-set`.

3. Create a `main.js` file that defines a new class named `Rocket` that takes a constructor argument `name` and assigns it to an instance property:

```
// main.js
class Rocket {
  constructor(name) {
    this.name = name;
  }
}
```

4. Create a class `RocketSet` file that creates a new map and assigns it as an instance property in the constructor:

```
// main.js
class RocketSet {
  constructor () {
    this.set = new WeakSet();
  }
}
```

5. Add an `add` method that checks the type of the `key` and `value` arguments. This method should throw if the argument types are incorrect; otherwise, set the pair as an entry on the map:

```
// main.js
class RocketSet {
  add (rocket) {
    if (!(rocket instanceof Rocket)) {
      throw new Error('Members of `RocketSet` must be of type
      `Rocket`');
    }

    this.set.add(rocket);
  }
}
```

6. Add a `has` method that returns `true` in the contained set has that entry:

```
// main.js
class RocketSiteMap {
  has (rocket) {
    return this.set.has(rocket);
    }
  }
}
```

7. Create a `main` function. Attempt to set various key and value pairs to an instance of `RocketSet`:

```
// main.js
export function main() {
  const rocketSet = new RocketSet();
  const saturnV = new Rocket('US: Saturn V');
  const falconHeavy = new Rocket('US: Falcon Heavy');
  const longMarch = new Rocket('Long March') ;
  rocketSet.add(saturnV);
  rocketSet.add(falconHeavy);
  rocketSet.add(longMarch);
  console.log(rocketSet) ;

  console.log('Set has Saturn V ',rocketSet.has(saturnV));
  console.log('Set has Falcon Heavy
  ',rocketSet.has(falconHeavy));
  console.log('Set has Long March ',rocketSet.has(longMarch));

  try {
    rocketSet.add('Buzz Lightyear');
  } catch (e) {
    console.error(e);
  }
}
```

8. Start your Python web server and open the following URL in your browser: `http://localhost:8000/`.

9. You should see the following output:

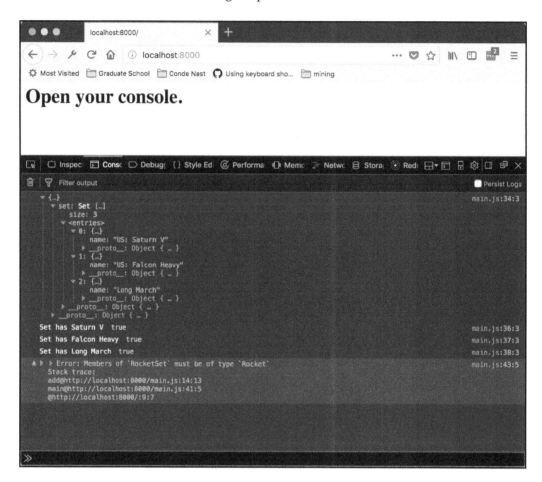

How it works...

From the implementation of the `add` method, we can see where the types of the argument are being checked. The `Rocket` instances behave like other instances we've seen in other recipes, and can be checked like the others. When the incorrect type is passed as an argument to add, one of the conditionals will trigger and an error will be thrown.

We don't have to check the types for the `has` method; it doesn't mutate the collection, and it will return `false` anyway if the argument isn't a `Rocket`.

Other Books You May Enjoy

If you enjoyed this book, you may be interested in these other books by Packt:

Hands-On Data Structures and Algorithms with JavaScript
Kashyap Mukkamala

ISBN: 978-1-78839-855-8

- Build custom Back buttons embedded within your application
- Build part of a basic JavaScript syntax parser and evaluator for an online IDE
- Build a custom activity user tracker for your application
- Generate accurate recommendations for credit card approval using Decision Trees
- Simplify complex problems using a graphs
- Increase the performance of an application using micro-optimizations

Learn ECMAScript - Second Edition
Mehul Mohan

ISBN: 978-1-78862-006-2

- Implement methods associated with objects as per the latest ECMAScript specification
- Make use of the latest features of ECMAScript
- Make use of many new APIs in HTML5 and modern JavaScript implementation
- Use SharedArrayBuffers for superfast concurrent and parallel programming
- Perform asynchronous programming with JavaScript
- Implement the best ways and practices to perform modular programming in JavaScript

Leave a review - let other readers know what you think

Please share your thoughts on this book with others by leaving a review on the site that you bought it from. If you purchased the book from Amazon, please leave us an honest review on this book's Amazon page. This is vital so that other potential readers can see and use your unbiased opinion to make purchasing decisions, we can understand what our customers think about our products, and our authors can see your feedback on the title that they have worked with Packt to create. It will only take a few minutes of your time, but is valuable to other potential customers, our authors, and Packt. Thank you!

Index

rest operator
  used, for obtaining head of array `264, 266`
  used, for obtaining tail of array `264, 266`

S

Sets
  creating, from existing data `300, 301`
  difference, finding `312`
  items, adding in `298, 299`
  items, deleting from `298, 299`
  reference `299`
setters
  used, for encapsulating values `178, 181`
SharedArray
  reading, from multiple Web Workers `126, 132`
SharedArrayBuffer
  creating `119, 120, 121`
  enabling, in Chrome `107, 109`
  enabling, in Firefox `106, 107`
  sending, to Web Worker `122, 126`
SimpleHTTPServer
  used, for hosting local static file server `12, 14`
singleton
  used, for managing instances `234, 236`
spread operator
  used, for combining arrays `266, 268`
  used, for combining objects `163, 165`
static methods
  used, for working with instances `181, 183`
steps
  defining, with template functions `216, 218, 220`
structure
  processing, with visitor pattern `228, 230, 232, 234`
super methods
  calling `197, 198, 199`
Symbol.for
  used, for creating global instance `273, 274`
Symbol
  used, for creating local instance `270, 271, 272`
  used, for simulating enums `275, 276`

T

tail of array

obtaining, rest operator used `264, 266`
template functions
  steps, defining with `216, 218, 220`
terminate
  workers, stopping with `116, 119`
throw
  used, for simulating abstract classes `211, 213`
tools
  used, for analyzing webpack bundles `47, 49`

U

union of two sets
  finding `306, 307, 309`

V

valid types
  reference `116`
values
  encapsulating, setters used `178, 181`
  producing, Array.map used `256, 258`
visitor pattern
  structure, processing `228, 230, 232, 234`

W

WeakMap
  creating, from existing data `289`
  entries, deleting from `286, 288`
  entries, setting `286, 288`
  reference `289`
  wrapper class, creating for `292`
WeakSet
  creating, from existing data `304, 306`
  items, adding in `302, 303`
  items, deleting from `302, 304`
Web Workers
  data, sending to `114, 116`
  messages, sending from `111, 113`
  messages, sending to `111, 113`
  SharedArray, reading from `132`
  SharedArrayBuffer, sending to `122, 126`
  work on separate threads, performing `109, 110, 111`
webpack bundles
  analyzing, tools used `47`

www.ingramcontent.com/pod-product-compliance
Lightning Source LLC
Chambersburg PA
CBHW080618060326
40690CB00021B/4742